The New Booktalker

The New Booktalker

Joni Richards Bodart
Editor

Volume **2**
Spring 1993

Libraries Unlimited, Inc.
Englewood, Colorado

LIBRARIES UNLIMITED, INC.
P.O. Box 6633
Englewood, CO 80155-6633

Library of Congress Cataloging-in-Publication Data

Suggested cataloging:

Bodart, Joni.
    The new booktalker.
    viii, 109 p. 22x28cm.
    Includes bibliographical references and indexes.
    ISBN 1-56308-087-7 Vol. 1 (Fall 1992)
    ISBN 1-56308-088-5 Vol. 2 (Spring 1993)
    ISSN 1064-7511
    1. Book talks. 2. Public relations--Libraries. 3. Books and reading.
  4. Libraries and readers.
  021.7B631
  Z716.3.B6

For information on contributing articles or booktalks, please contact:
    Dr. Joni Richards Bodart, Editor
    The New Booktalker
    P.O. Box 72
    Littleton, CO 80160
    (303) 972-1846 or Fax (303) 972-3221

For advertising information, please contact:
    Marketing Director
    Libraries Unlimited, Inc.
    P.O. Box 6633
    Englewood, CO 80155-6633
    (303) 770-1220 or 1-800-237-6124

Contents

Booktalking the Curriculum by Lesley S. J. Farmer

Old Reliables

The New Booktalker

Volume 2   Spring 1993

From the Editor

Oh, the joys of living ahead of oneself! You're reading this in spring 1993, but I'm writing it in October 1992, and the first issue of *The New Booktalker* isn't even back from the printer yet. There's no way for me to know yet what you thought of that first issue, or what you'd like to see in the second. I can't have comments and letters from readers when no one's read it yet. I haven't rejoiced or agonized over reviews, either—that will come later. But nevertheless, the second issue is due at Libraries Unlimited today, "and not a day later," I've been told. So here I am, writing in the dark and remembering having to produce the second issue of *The Booktalker* in exactly the same state.

But while some things are the same, others are different. In this issue, we begin to include review citations on the titles in the "Promising Newcomers" section. You'll notice, however, that not all the titles in that section have citations. That's because I am using up talks submitted on the old form, which did not include a request for citations. Also, some talks submitted on the new form had no citations, either because someone didn't take the time to look up reviews or because no reviews were available. Change doesn't always happen overnight, and I hope you will be patient with us as we learn new habits.

Another new feature is "The Last Word," a chance for readers to respond to what they see—or don't see—in *NBT*. There's nothing like starting a feature before there's anything to include in it! So when Jeff Blair's satirical "The Booktalker's Top Ten List, with Apologies to David Letterman" came in recently, it seemed like the perfect solution. I hope you enjoy it and that you'll want to contribute something of your own for our next issue.

"Talking with the Talkers" is also new to *NBT*, although it appeared several times in *BT*. It gives you a chance to meet the people and personalities behind the booktalks. I hope you enjoy this section too.

Deadlines crept up on me this fall, and I had to make several frantic telephone calls to request articles that people had volunteered to write "sometime." I am delighted with the caliber of the results. Mary Ann Capan, who has added to the scant research on booktalking with her master's thesis, discusses the results here. When she asked if I would be interested in an article on her research, she commented that *NBT* seemed to be the logical place for booktalking research results. I agreed, and I hope you do as well.

Patty Campbell is not only a friend of long standing, she is also a talented writer and editor who has put her distinctive stamp on the Twayne Young Adult Authors series. Her article introduces the series, but unfortunately the books themselves arrived too late to be included in my final shipment to contributors before this deadline, so talks on them will be in the next issue. I've done a talk on Patty's *Presenting Robert Cormier* to give you a taste of what's in store for you. In addition, there are booktalks on 20 other individual and collective biographies and fictionalized biographies to help you entice kids to discover examples of how others have succeeded and how they themselves can succeed.

If you are among the booktalkers who spend hours doing booktalks for six or seven months a year, Bette Ammon and Gale Sherman's article on using props with booktalks may be just the thing to give your talks a new twist—for the benefit of both you and your audience! I can remember getting bored with the same old thing and wishing I could think of something new to do, other than read another 20 or 30 new books and write talks on them. Props might just be the answer. Bette's article suggests many ideas, and I know you can take it from there.

Speaking of new ideas, Lesley Farmer's article on using booktalking as part of the curriculum is just full of them! If you know teachers who haven't been converted into booktalking fans yet—who don't want to "waste" their valuable class time—put some of Lesley's ideas into action and show those doubting Thomases just how much their students and their curriculum can benefit from a few booktalks.

In this issue, for the first time in *NBT*, we have three sections of talks on different types of books, just as we did several times in *BT*. I've already mentioned the biography section. In addition to that, we have groups of talks on poetry books and on short story and drama collections. I hope the talks in these sections will give you some ideas on how to approach booktalking these kinds of books.

As I mentioned before, deadlines for this issue were upon me before I even realized it. That's because I had accepted a job running book fairs in elementary and middle schools for a local book wholesaler. I learned many things, not least among them that it is not possible to work full-time and produce a book every six months. So we parted company, leaving me with six weeks of book fair experience under my belt, and my once-again unemployed status to give me time to think about the experience. As a result, I gained some new knowledge about what and why kids read or don't read—or maybe just some old knowledge relearned.

Kids don't read what they're supposed to read. And the older they get, the less frequently they read what they are told to read. They read what their friends tell them about and what those friends recommend.

They read books that scare them, so they will have some idea of how to confront the far more frightening things they must deal with in real life. They want—*need*—literary monsters in all shapes and sizes to help them cope with the real monsters in their families, their neighborhoods, and their schools.

They read books that help them figure out what to do about situations that they have no clue how to deal with. And they also read books that, instead of helping them confront reality, help them escape from it for an hour or two, because everyone needs some time off.

They read books whose authors they've met, or want to meet, authors who have responded to their letters and their questions. When they find a book they connect with and have read or want to read over and over, they frequently decide to read all the books written by that person. And when they find a favorite book, they want to own it. Parents' comments about, "You've read that book three times, why don't you buy one you haven't read?" may have little or no effect. The triumph in the face of a fifth-grader who has succeeded in persuading his parent to buy *Hatchet*, and the reluctance in the face of another whose parent just purchased a new, unread, and untrusted title for her, make it undeniably clear what they want to read.

There are few certain ways to determine ahead of time what books will sell in a school and which other titles

will be repacked days later, completely untouched. Some titles are always popular: Bruce Coville's My Teacher series, the three titles in the Scary Stories series, the Babysitter's Club, the American Girls, Ninja Turtles, Nancy Drew, and Hardy Boys series, and the Berenstain Bears.

For every standard title, though, there are a few surprises. A teacher read *Don't Open the Door* to the entire second grade in one school, and we sold out not only our fair supply, but also the stock in the warehouse. No one could ever remember selling even one copy previously!

One elementary school librarian had met Joan Lowery Nixon, and the fifth-graders couldn't get enough of her books, even the suspense stories written for young adults. (Yet this same librarian asked me to remove the Paula Danziger titles from the sale, saying that Danziger's negative views of parents and men were unacceptable.)

Kids at yet another school all but wiped out the stock of the three Wayside School books. A stunned stockman in the warehouse commented, "*More*?? But I sent you 10 yesterday!" This school's librarian had no idea why they were so popular. They sell well other places, but we sold at least 20 copies of each of the titles at this school—definitely a record!

Nevertheless, it's important to remember that these examples do not contradict my earlier assertion that kids do not read—or at least do not read voraciously—books that are good for them or books that teachers, parents, and librarians make them read. "Make" is the key word here—in fact, it's always been the key word. I *still* haven't read *My Antonia*, although my mother spent two weeks trying to force it on me when I was a high school sophomore with a bad case of flu. Maybe if it hadn't had those deadly woodcut illustrations. . . .

Kids read books that they are *inspired* to read, and that's where booktalking comes in. When booktalking is a part of the equation, it's no longer an adult making a kid read a book—it's an adult making a kid *want* to read a book. There's a vast difference between the two! A single fan of *The Dollhouse Murders* can convert her classmates, and make it a school best-seller, but a booktalk can create that first fan.

Teachers and librarians who are enthusiastic about books, and communicate that enthusiasm, are sure to create enthusiastic readers. The librarian who was a Nixon fan had boys in her school happily reading suspense stories written for (or at least narrated by) girls. She didn't do this by telling the kids what they would learn from the books, but by telling them—and their teachers—about her own experience with the books.

A story I heard her tell many times during the three days I spent in her library involved her husband's reaction to reading the first of the Orphan Train series. He'd picked it up because she had it at home over the Christmas break and had mentioned that it was good. He started reading it in the bathtub and ended up sitting in a tubful of ice-cold water to finish it. When he did, he came storming out of the bathroom, furious at the author. "She didn't finish the story! I want to know what happened to Mike!" He was glad to learn that there were other books, and demanded the next one immediately. But it was Christmas vacation, the school was locked, and he had to wait impatiently for January. You can guess which titles were the first checked out when the library opened its doors again. (I'm not sure why they didn't just go to the nearest public library, but I hated to ruin a good story by asking the question.) Although this story seems like it might work better with adults than with kids, I nevertheless heard kids ask about and comment on "the book your husband read in the tub," and that title was another of our top sellers at that school.

Kids of all ages also reread what has been read to them. Gary Paulsen's *Hatchet* has been read in more classrooms than I can count, and has converted young readers and nonreaders from all over the country into ardent fans. I don't think I will ever forget the mother who, although she couldn't afford it, bought a hardback copy of *The River* because her son had never read a book in his life until his teacher read *Hatchet*, and he'd decided to read it again himself. They came in to buy him a copy of *Hatchet*, and I mentioned the sequel. When I saw the mother's dismay at the hardback cost, I suggested that they write down the title and check it out from their local public library. But that wasn't good enough. This mother wanted her son to read, and if the book he'd immediately set his heart on cost more, then she'd just find the money somewhere. They had to put back two other titles they'd picked up, but they went home with *The River*. There's no doubt in my mind that this boy will become a reader; his mother knows how important owning books—and owning books you are passionate about—can be. The next time Gary's

in Denver, I'll bet that boy will be in line for an autograph in his well-read copies of *Hatchet* and *The River*.

Don't tell kids to read. Inspire them to read. Persuade them to read. Introduce them to the people they'll meet and the adventures they can share in books. Show them a little bit of what they will be missing if they don't read the books you tell them about. You don't have to convince every kid in a school or a class to read—you just have to convince a few. They'll finish the job for you when they tell their friends, who will then tell their friends, about the books you talked about.

Booktalks don't demand, they don't require, they don't force. They persuade, they convince, they motivate, and eventually they convert kids into readers. They are one of our most powerful tools to ensure that our audiences believe in the importance of reading. Because of that, and because of your example, kids will understand and believe in the importance of libraries.

Well, I'll step down from my soapbox now. But if you'd like to hear more, or to hear in detail about how to do booktalks and set up a booktalking program in your school, do let me know. I enjoy doing workshops and lectures and creating a whole new group of booktalking converts!

Finally, those of you in school libraries may want to take a look at my columns in *The Book Report* and *Library Talk* that started in last year's November/December issue of both magazines. Because the magazines' readerships are different from that of *NBT*, my focus there is slightly different, and, of course, the columns will include information and talks that you won't be able to find elsewhere.

I think that's about all. You know what to expect in this issue, and I've had my time on my soapbox. Now it's time for the real reason you picked this up—booktalks and ideas about how to do them and how to use them. Have fun, and Happy Booktalking until next time!

—Joni Richards Bodart

Know Your Ps & Qs

P (Popularity)
4P A book everyone wants to read
3P A booktalk on this title will excite most
     people's interest
2P A good booktalk may help sell this book
1P For those readers who are particularly
     interested in a subject

Q (Quality)
4Q Exceptional!
3Q A good story with some faults
2Q Many problems; booktalk only because
     of its popularity

The P and Q rating system is adapted from Voice of Youth Advocates.

Storytelling Resources
from Libraries Unlimited

Folk Stories of the Hmong
Peoples of Laos, Thailand, and Vietnam

Norma J. Livo and Dia Cha

Recommended.–The Book Report

A beautiful book and a real labor of love.–Voice of Youth Advocates

The first collection of authentic Hmong tales to be translated into the English language and made available to story lovers. Includes a description of Hmong history, culture, and folklore, with full-color photographs of Hmong dress and needlework.

1991 xii, 135p. ISBN 0-87287-854-6 color plates
$22.00

Images of a People
Tlingit Myths and Legends

Mary Helen Pelton and Jackie DiGennaro

This captivating new collection of 22 legends introduces you to the Tlingit culture and people, their history, land, and traditional art forms. Tales range from creation myths to religious stories and more. Illustrations by Tlingit artist Ts'anak lend visual depth.

1992 xvii, 170p. ISBN 0-87287-918-6 color plates
$22.00 ($26.50f)

Hyena and the Moon
and Other Stories to Tell from Kenya

Heather McNeil Cromer

Enchanting tales that have been gathered from 7 of the more than 40 ethnic tribes of Kenya are brought to you both as original translations and expanded, ready-to-use retellings. Cultural and historical background information about the tribes, color photos of Kenyan storytellers and the animals portrayed in the stories, notes on the stories, lists of further resources, and tips for retelling will make this collection especially useful.

Fall 1993 ca.160p. ISBN 1-56308-169-5 color plates
$23.00

Magic Minutes
Quick Read-Alouds for Every Day

Pat Nelson

Guaranteed to spread a special magic over listeners and bring many minutes of enchantment to all, this collection of 170 short, short stories (1-3 minutes) celebrates tried and true wisdom from around the world, as well as old time humor and new time heroes. A delightful collection of folk literature from many different cultures, nonfiction tales from history, math and science problems or anecdotes, biographical sketches, and real life stories. Seasonally arranged for your convenience.

1993 xv, 151p. paper
ISBN 0-87287-996-8
$18.50

Storytelling for Young Adults
Techniques and Treasury

Gail de Vos

Will be valued by all who count young adults among their listeners.–RQ

A creative approach for drawing out from young people a variety of their talents.–Curriculum Review

This guide and resource for those who work with young adults shows how storytelling with young adults encourages the development of insight into motives and patterns of human behavior. It also contains a valuable bibliography of 120 stories particularly suited to young adults aged 13-18. Stories are summarized, timed, and arranged by subject.

1991 x, 169p. ISBN 0-87287-832-5
$24.50

Story Play
Costumes, Cooking, Music, and More for Young Children

Joyce Harlow

Popular fairy-tale themes provide the basis for this enchanting, integrated curriculum activity book. "Little Red Riding Hood," "The Three Little Pigs," and other traditional children's stories are extended with group and individual experiences in drama, literature, writing, art activities, science, games, cooking, music, and mathematics. Each fairy-tale theme includes directions for a variety of open-ended, developmentally appropriate activities.

1992 xii, 200p. 8 1/2 x 11 paper
ISBN 1-56308-037-0
$19.00

Story Play Music

Experience the sounds and sensations of tiptoeing through a jungle, painting with a feather, or climbing a magic beanstalk! This companion tape to *Story Play*, designed to accompany the fairy-tale themes included in the book, provides a beautiful and relaxing background to the book's activities.

1992 Order no. X370
$10.00

Recipe for Success: Increase Circulation Through Booktalking

By Mary Ann Capan
Western Illinois University, Macomb, Illinois

For many people, reading is the most satisfying experience in the world, outweighing Mom, baseball, and apple pie. Through reading, one can travel through time; explore the world's past, present, and future; learn something new. One can gain insight into and empathy for a character or vicariously experience a situation discovered in a book. Motivating young people to become lifetime learners and readers is a major goal of most teachers and librarians. One method used to create an interest in books and reading is the booktalk.

In December of 1985, Joni Richards Bodart completed her doctoral dissertation, which examined the effects of booktalking presentations on the circulation of the books presented and the effects of the booktalks on the reading attitudes of a group of senior high school students. Her study results showed that booktalking does indeed increase circulation.[1] As a result of her dissertation, Bodart made 10 recommendations, one of which was to study the effectiveness of booktalking on an audience of a different age level.[2] With this recommendation in mind, I conducted a study similar to Bodart's dissertation as a research project for my MLS from Northern Illinois University.[3]

In the spring of 1989, I was completing my fourteenth year of teaching in the Moline (Illinois) Public Schools. The last six had been at John Deere Junior High School. Principal Burt Ringquist and librarian Donna De-Volder enthusiastically supported the project from beginning to end. As a matter of fact, Donna ended up carrying a large portion of the project on her own, because I took a teaching position with Western Illinois University in August of that year.

We began with a master list of books consisting of all the books on the "Honor Sampling" list from the third edition of *Literature for Today's Young Adults* by Alleen Pace Nilsen and Kenneth L. Donelson. These titles were compared to the holdings at John Deere Junior High School. Books that were not a part of Deere's collection were eliminated from the master list, as were any books that were not novels. Donna then eliminated from the list any books that she had booktalked during the previous school year. Together we studied the remaining titles on the list and chose 20 that we felt would be appropriate for the eighth-grade readers at John Deere. This final list became the titles used in the study.

During the summer of 1989, Donna wrote booktalks for the 20 books in the study. At the same time, circulation records of these titles were totaled for each of the three previous years.

By the end of the first nine weeks of the 1989–90 school year, Donna had presented booktalks on two titles to each of the ten eighth-grade English classes at John Deere. After six months, the circulation records of the titles used in the study were totaled for the period from November 1989 to May 1990. The circulation records for the three years before the booktalks (1986–87, 1987–88, and 1988–89) were then compared with the 1989–90 statistics.

The circulation records of the titles used in this study appear in Table 1. Fifteen of twenty books were checked out more during the 1989–90 school year than in the previous school year. Three of the books were checked out the same number of times both years, while two of the books saw decreased circulation. Comparing the 1989–90 and 1987–88 school years, 14 of the books increased in circulation, 5 decreased, and 1 book's circulation remained the same. Comparing the 1989–90 and the 1986–87 school years, 16 of the books were checked out more during 1989–90 than in 1986–87. One book was checked out less, and three books had identical circulation records.

Table 1
Circulation Records of Titles Used in This Study

Title	School Years			
	86/87	87/88	88/89	89/90
After the First Death	1	2	1	3[a]
The Contender	0	3	1	1
Deathwatch	0	2	1	4
A Formal Feeling	0	1	1	3
House of Stairs	1	1	0	3
Is That You, Miss Blue?	0	0	0	1
Izzy, Willy-Nilly	0	0	3	6
The Last Mission	5	6	5	5
M. C. Higgins, the Great	6	7	10	1
The Pigman	2	0	0	3
Remembering the Good Times	2	3	3	2
Rumble Fish	3	1	3	3
Run Softly, Go Fast	0	0	0	1
Sixteen	0	0	1	2
The Slave Dancer	0	3	0	2
Sounder	0	1	0	12
Stranger with My Face	3	5	6	21
Summer of My German Soldier	1	0	0	2
Where the Lillies Bloom	7	8	1	8
Wild in the World	0	0	0	2
Totals	31	43	36	85

[a]Book was due on February 9, 1990, and had not been returned by the end of the study.

Table 2 compares the average circulation after the booktalk presentations to the circulation during the three previous years. Circulation increased for 16 of the 20 titles. Four titles decreased in circulation. However, two of these four books saw a decrease of only 0.33, and only one title saw a decrease of 0.67. The only title that showed a significant decrease in circulation was *M.C. Higgins, the Great*. During the 1989–90 school year, this book was checked out only once. During the three previous years, this title circulated 6, 7, and 10 times.

Table 2
Change in Circulation of Titles Used in This Study

Title	3 Yr. Average Circulation	School Year 89/90	Change in Circulation
After the First Death	1.33	3[a]	+1.67
The Contender	1.33	1	-0.33
Deathwatch	1.33	4	+2.67
A Formal Feeling	0.50	3	+2.50
House of Stairs	0.50	3	+2.50
Is That You, Miss Blue?	0.00	1	+1.00
Izzy, Willy-Nilly	0.75	6	+5.25
The Last Mission	5.33	5	-0.33
M. C. Higgins, the Great	7.67	1	-6.67
The Pigman	0.67	3	+2.33
Remembering the Good Times	2.67	2	-0.67
Rumble Fish	2.33	3	+0.67
Run Softly, Go Fast	0.00	1	+1.00
Sixteen	0.33	2	+1.67
The Slave Dancer	1.00	2	+1.00
Sounder	0.33	12	+11.67
Stranger with My Face	4.67	21	+16.33
Summer of My German Soldier	0.33	2	+1.67
Where the Lillies Bloom	5.33	8	+2.67
Wild in the World	0.00	2	+2.00
Totals	36.67	85	+48.33

[a] Book was due on Feb. 9, 1990, and had not been returned by the end of the study.

Three books in the study showed a large increase in circulation: *Stranger with My Face*, *Sounder*, and *Izzy, Willy-Nilly*. Lois Duncan's supernatural mystery *Stranger with My Face* was checked out 21 times during the 1989–90 school year, after having been checked out only 3, 5, and 6 times during the previous three years. *Sounder* was checked out 12 times during the study year, yet its circulation for the three previous years was only 0, 1, and 0. Cynthia Voigt's novel *Izzy, Willy-Nilly* was checked out six times during 1989–90. During 1988–89, it was checked out only three times, and prior to that it had not been checked out at all.

Overall, the 20 books used in this study were checked out a total of 31 times during the 1986–87 school year, 43 times during 1987–88, 36 times during 1988–89, and 85 times during 1989–90. (One of the books used in the study, *After the First Death* by Robert Cormier, was checked out by one student, and although it was due on February 9, 1990, it had not been returned as of May 15, 1990.)

The limitations of this study should be noted. If similar studies are done, and these factors eliminated, circulation statistics could increase even more dramatically. Donna, the librarian in this study, did only two booktalks per class. All but one of the titles were available only in hardback, and most of the dust jackets had been removed by a previous librarian. The library had only one copy of each book, so students were required to wait to read most of the titles. Booktalking was the only promotion done on these books, other than the students' "grapevine," or word-of-mouth recommendations.

The results of this study support the hypothesis that the circulation of young adult fiction titles will increase if junior high students are exposed to booktalking presentations. The results also support the findings of others who have done similar research, formally and informally.

Library science professors who teach courses in young adult literature should include information on how to do booktalks, how to set up booktalking programs in local schools, and how to support these programs. Having a solid background in young adult literature is one thing; having the skill and technique necessary to write and deliver booktalks to persuade teenagers to read those books is another. Professors who teach children's literature also need to be aware of the power of booktalking, because the same techniques that persuade teenagers to read can be used just as effectively with grade-school students.

Courses in public libraries also should include information on booktalking. Administrators need to know about this technique's effectiveness in increasing circulation and library use statistics. Public librarians who work with children and young adults can provide booktalking services to schools, either in addition to or in cooperation with the school librarians. Booktalking can help forge a strong working relationship between schools and the public library and strengthen their efforts to work together for the benefit of the youth of their community.

English teachers at the secondary level also need to be aware of the power of booktalking and its ability to convince young people to read for recreation. Secondary English teachers' courses in young adult literature should include information on booktalking, just as children's literature courses are required for most elementary and early childhood education majors.

This study and others show that booktalking does increase reading among junior and senior high school students. Booktalking can and should be a vital part of the total literature spectrum presented to potential teachers and librarians. It does affect literature selection and can make reading a pleasure.

Notes

1. Bodart, Joni. "The Effect of a Booktalking Presentation of Selected Titles on the Attitude Toward Reading of Senior High School Students and on the Circulation of These Titles in the High School Library." (Ph.D. diss., Texas Woman's University, 1985), 65.

2. Ibid., 103–4.

3. Capan, Mary Ann. "A Study of the Effect of Booktalk Presentations of Selected Titles on the Circulation of These Titles in a Junior High School Library." (Unpublished research project, Northern Illinois University, 1990).

Promising Newcomers

Note: Promising Newcomers includes books published from 1991–1992.

📖 Adrift

Allan Baillie. Viking, 1992. 119p. Hardbound (ISBN 0-670-84474-8) $14.00. **Grades 3–8. 3Q, 3P.**
Reviewed in: SLJ, 5/92; Bklst, 3/15/92; PW, 5/4/92.

Flynn may be young, but he's had a lot to live through in his short life. He's nearly drowned, his little sister Sally was almost killed in a bicycle wreck, and their family lost their farm because of the drought. But none of those disasters can even come close to the mess he's gotten himself and Sally into now.

Flynn may be young, but his imagination is as good, or better, than any adult's. He and Sally aren't playing on the beach while their parents entertain boring relatives, no way. They're in the seventeenth century, pirates rampaging over the high seas. Flynn is the captain, Sally, the loyal cabin boy, and an old wooden crate, their pirate ship. But when they realize that their ship has taken to the high seas in reality, the seventeenth century vanishes, and they are just two frightened children. They had been so involved in their game that they hadn't realized the crate was no longer stuck in the sand on the beach, but floating out to sea, too far for anyone to hear their cries for help.

Flynn may be young, but he knows when he's in trouble—and he *is* in trouble now. They're adrift on the ocean, two children and their terrified cat, at the mercy of the weather and the sharks that soon begin to circle the crate. Will someone find them before they die of exposure or the sharks discover that they can bite through the wooden crate?

Flynn is young, but will he and his sister ever get any older?

—Cynthia Cordes
Onondaga County Public Library, Syracuse, NY

📖 Alaska: Pioneer Stories of a Twentieth-Century Frontier

Luree Miller and Scott Miller. Nonfiction. Dutton, 1991. 116p. Hardbound (ISBN 0-525-65050-4) $14.95. **Grades 9–12, adults. 4Q, 3P.**

The Great Land—Alaska—is not just a location or a landscape, it is a state of mind. Surviving there demands independence, frankness, openness, and self-reliance.

Alaska welcomes those looking for a new start. It's a land of pioneers, a land where each individual is valuable and important in the struggle to live in a sometimes overwhelming environment.

Two of those pioneers were Frank and Mary Miller, who left their home in Montana in 1906 to search for gold in Alaska. They spent their first winter in a one-room, sod-roofed cabin, while temperatures dropped as low as 40 to 60 degrees below zero.

Millie Dodson washed almost a hundred diapers every week in that same chilling cold. She hung the diapers on the line to freeze and stacked them like firewood outside the cabin, to be brought in and thawed as she needed them.

Alaska pioneers braved the 1964 earthquake and reclaimed their property from the Exxon Valdez oil spill. They fought for their land and their future. These are their stories.

—Helen Schlichting
Sac Community School, Sac City, IA

📖 All but Alice

Phyllis Reynolds Naylor. Atheneum, 1992. 151p. Hardbound (ISBN 0-689-31773-5) $13.95. **Grades 5–8. 4Q, 4P.**

Alice is back! Alice Kathleen McKinley, who's been "in Agony," "in Rapture," and who "Reluctantly" started junior high, is now in seventh grade with her friends Pamela, Elizabeth, and Patrick.

By the time Alice has been in seventh grade for a few months, she's realized how important it is to fit in with the crowd. Having her ears pierced really made Alice feel like she belonged, and besides, it meant she could join the earring club and go with the other members to buy earrings at the mall every week. She even joined the All Star Fan Club, although she didn't think it would be all that much fun writing fan letters to rock stars—but all the girls in her new crowd were doing it, so Alice went along. She also ended up in the school talent show, too, because all her friends were in it. But while she was busy being part of the

┌───┐
Abbreviations of Review Journals/Sources

Bklst	= *Booklist*
HB	= *Hornbook*
NYTBR	= *New York Times Books Review*
PW	= *Publishers Weekly*
Science Bks & Films	= *Science Books & Films*
SLJ	= *School Library Journal*
Utne	= *Utne Reader*
VOYA	= *Voice of Youth Advocates*
└───┘

right crowd, her old friends were becoming strangers, and Alice wasn't sure she liked that.

And school wasn't the only place where things didn't go the way Alice had expected them to. There were problems at home, too. Her big brother, Lester, couldn't decide which of his girlfriends he liked better, her father was dating her gorgeous Language Arts teacher, Miss Summers, and Alice had all kinds of questions she couldn't answer. Questions like: What could be in that little teeny gift box her dad was going to give Miss Summers for Valentine's Day? How long could a brother be in love with two girls at the same time and not become mentally deranged? What did her dad really put in his homemade soup? Should a girl with a talent for fake barfing use her abilities indiscriminately? Last but not least, should you accept candy from a boy? If Alice had a mother to talk to, things would be different. But since she didn't, she just had to muddle through on her own.

Spend a little time with Alice—you may find out you have a lot in common with her!

—*Mary McNeil*
Shimek Elementary School, Iowa City, IA

Alone on the Great Wall

William Lindesay. Nonfiction. Fulcrum, 1991. 218p. Paperbound (ISBN 1-55591-079-3) $14.95. **Grades 9–12, adults. 3Q, 2P.**

Happiness has many forms. For William Lindesay, after a day of running along the Great Wall of China, happiness was a bowl of noodles and a place to wash his socks. Most often it would be in a small village, where the townspeople welcomed him. Those were wonderful times of sharing and talking and enjoying the constant curiosity of children. In fact, the kind folk of the People's Republic of China were the real heroes of Will's journey as he ran the length of the Great Wall. Without their help, it's unlikely that he would ever have achieved his goal. He traveled light and was susceptible to illness and injury. In spite of his mental and physical stamina, there were times when he had to be carried to a cot and nursed back to health over a number of days. When he was able to run again, the people of the village who had cared for him sent him off on the next leg of his journey with a tribute to "our English friend" written in beautiful Chinese script. Will carried with him not only the scraps of paper, but also his memories of their faces, their smiles, and the way they had cared for him. Those memories gave him as much strength and comfort as any blister cream ever did.

The people of China helped Will, but the government seemed to do everything it could to harass him and block his way. Even though he carried a passport, visa, and letters of introduction, he sometimes had to make an unplanned detour to get a paper signed or show his paperwork to yet another official. Perhaps that's to be expected, though, when you're determined to do what no one else has done, even if you've been told it's impossible for a Westerner to run the length of the Great Wall of China.

Run with Will, and let him introduce you to the people who helped him, the people who hindered him, and one very special woman who married him.

—*Mark Anderson*
Fairfax County Public Library, Fairfax, VA

Anna and the Cat Lady

Barbara M. Joose. Illustrated by Gretchen Will Mayo. HarperCollins, 1992. 170p. Hardbound (ISBN 0-06-020242-4) $14.00. **Grades 3–6. 3Q, 3P.**

Hi! My name is Anna. My friend Bethie and I have this Adventurer's Club. We have our meetings in a cow tunnel. You don't know what that is?! Well, here in Door County, Wisconsin, there are big cement tubes that go underneath the highway. Cows use them to go from one pasture to another so they don't have to cross the road. They make a great hide-out for a secret club.

But even though we make lots of plans, Bethie and I hardly ever have any *real* adventures. The only really, truly adventure we had was when we decided to explore the old deserted house up the road that was supposed to be haunted. Boy, were we scared when we heard weird screeching sounds coming from a hole in the floorboards. It was sure a relief to find out that it was only a trapped kitten, and not a ghost! And that's when the adventure started to get seriously out of control, because when we tried to get the kitten out of the hole, we fell in ourselves, and couldn't get out! If Mrs. Sarafiny, the Cat Lady, hadn't come along with her six cats, I don't know how we would ever have gotten out.

Afterwards, Bethie and I decided to visit Mrs. Sarafiny. She was so nice, and seemed to be all alone, except for her cats. But the more we talked to her, the more worried about her we got. She talked about Martians who were stealing her food, and sometimes she even had to eat cat food—gross! And she didn't just say weird things, sometimes she did weird things, too. We knew we had to do something—but what?

—*Mary MacNeil*
Shimek Elementary School, Iowa City, IA

Aunt Maria

Diana Wynne Jones. Greenwillow, 1992.
214p. Hardbound (ISBN 0-688-10611-0)
$13.95. **Grades 5–8. 4Q, 3P.**
Reviewed in: SLJ, 10/91, p. 142; NYTBR,
4/19/92, p. 16; PW, 8/16/91, p. 59.

"You murderess!" Chris snarled. "What!" Aunt Maria said faintly. She sat in her afternoon chair, both canes by her side, staring at Chris.

"You killed Dad, because he found out about the green box and tried to get it back, didn't you? I don't know what you did to him, except I know he didn't go off the cliff like everyone was supposed to think—."

"How dare you!" said Aunt Maria. "I've never killed anything in all my life!"

But Chris wouldn't stop. "You got rid of Lavinia because she knew too much, and Anthony so you could get hold of that box and the power in—."

Aunt Maria stood, pointing one of her canes at Chris. "By the power vested in me," she said, "go on four feet in the shape your nature makes you, young man." And she thumped the other cane on the floor.

Chris wailed, folded up, and hit the floor. His hands shrank and bent, his thumbs traveled up his arms and grew claws. His whole body seethed and became a different thing—a thing that snarled and fought and backed out of Chris's clothes.

I stood frozen in horror. This visit with Aunt Maria that had been so deadly dull had now become a nightmare. What was *happening* in this village of zombie men and clone-like children? What *was* Aunt Maria? My brain was paralyzed. How could I save Chris? Why doesn't my mother even notice he's gone? How can I ever stop Aunt Maria?

—Julie Bray
Jasper County Public Library, Rensselaer, IN

Back in the Blue House

Jeff Giles. Ticknor & Fields, 1992. 214p. Hardbound (ISBN 0-395-60843-0) $19.95. **Adults. 3Q, 3P.**

Hi, my name is Jeff Giles, and this is the story of my family. It's about my father, an airline pilot who loved flight attendants. After their divorce, he tried to get my mother back by riding a lawn mower around and around the house. My mother called the police.

It's about my mother, who became addicted to York Peppermint Patties after she divorced my father. She'd call me on my phone from her room only a few feet away just to talk about nothing in particular.

It's about my sister, the teenage terror, who was heavily into collage and booze and arguing with my mother, stepmother, father, me, and anyone else who crossed her path.

And it's about me—I lived through it all, the arguments the police had to break up, the boredom of living in a small town, and the good times, because there actually were some good times. I lived through it, and I lived to write a book about it all.

—Nancy A. Weitendorf
Oxford Land Library, Oxford, OH

Begin the World Again

Bettie Cannon. Charles Scribner's Sons, 1991.
181p. Hardbound (ISBN 0-684-19292-6)
$13.95. **Grades 7–12. 4Q, 2P.**

On the night before her sixteenth birthday, Lake catches her mother Selene leaving home. Selene's going to Nashville to become a country-and-western singer, and she's leaving behind not only Lake, but also Lake's father and all the members of their commune, her whole family. She's starting her life over again.

Lake has always wondered what it would be like to live outside the commune, to have things and space she could call her own, like her friends at school have. She also wonders what it would be like to have a boyfriend. She's attracted to Sun Dog, a dark-haired young man who wants to join their commune. But when Sun Dog leaves and Lake discovers that she can't go to high school the next year, she leaves too. She borrows bus fare from a friend and goes to live with Grand, Selene's mother. Now she, too, can start her life all over again. She can go to high school and live in a regular house like other teenagers do.

But all that changes when Selene shows up again, on her way to California, and wants Lake to come with her. Lake loves her mother, but is being with her worth giving up her dream of a new life, a normal life?

—Mary Hedge
La Porte County Public Library, La Porte, IN

Between Two Worlds

Joan Lingard. Dutton, 1991. 186p. Hardbound (ISBN 0-525-67360-1) $14.95. **Grades 5–12. 4Q, 3P.**

After years of starvation and fear during World War II, the Petersons have finally arrived in Canada. Their sponsor has found a job for Lukas and a place for them to live. But all their plans are shattered when Lukas has a massive heart attack at the train station and cannot go to work. Suddenly it seems like nothing can go right—everyone and everything seems to have turned against them, including the bitterly cold Canadian winter.

Hugo and Astrid, the 18-year-old twins, are torn between wanting to adapt to Canadian ways in their new homeland and remembering their friends and Hugo's fiancée left behind in Europe. Even 12-year-old Tomas, who loves cars and all things new, is having trouble adapting to strange customs like sending Valentine cards.

The Petersons are a strong and loving family. They have survived World War II and escaped to safety in Canada. Will that be enough?

—*Bette Ammon*
Missoula Public Library, Missoula, MT

📖 Bingo Brown's Guide to Romance

Betsy Byars. Viking, 1992. 115p. Hardbound (ISBN 0-670-84491-8) $14.00. **Grades 5–8. 3Q, 4P.**

Do you know Bingo Brown? He's the kid whose journals are full of strange questions and even stranger answers.

In Bingo's newest book, he decides to spare his new baby brother the heartache of romance by preparing for him a complete guide to romance, presented in Bingo's own very special question-and-answer style. When Jamie grows up, he'll be able to use this guide to cook up the perfect romance, just like a chef uses a recipe to cook a wonderful dish. But before he can give it to Jamie, Bingo has to test out his recipe himself. He gathers all the ingredients together:

one basket of dirty laundry
one Declaration of Independence T-shirt
one enlarging girl
one one-way street
one Piggly-Wiggly grocery store
a pinch of photocopied love letter
a dash of worm-brain.

The directions are: Mix together and keep mixing.

Does Bingo's recipe work? Is it the recipe for the perfect romance, or for something a lot less pleasant?

—*Tracy Revel*
Sussex Central Middle School, Millsboro, DE

📖 Blue Between the Clouds

Stephen Wunderli. Holt, 1992. 114p. Hardbound (ISBN 0-80501772-0) $13.95. **Grades 4–8. 4Q, 3P.**
Reviewed in: SLJ, 6/92; PW, 3/30/92.

Remember Tom Sawyer and Huck Finn? Well, Matt Canton and Two Moons are just like them—best friends and virtually inseparable. They've been friends since the moment they met—in a fight on the first day of school in September 1939. Matt's mother is determined to make sure the two boys learn to get along, and so she decides that Two Moons should live with them for the next year.

It was a match made in heaven—or maybe someplace a little warmer than that—because Matt, a small-town boy with a craving for adventure and mischief, and Two Moons, an Indian boy anxious to learn the ways of the white world, can together raise enough hell to empty a hen house! If the two aren't stealing Ma's biscuits through an open window, they're pitching at bats down by the holding pond, or getting into egg-throwing or slingshot fights with Matt's sister Esther.

But when they really get down to serious business, they dream of flying, of soaring through the sky, free and untethered. So when Pa uncovers the remains of an old World War I flier in the old barn, the boys can think of nothing else except getting it into the air again. But they don't know how to fly, much less repair an airplane—all their flying hours have been in their imaginations. But Uncle Emmett might be able to help them. He was never quite right after the war, but Pa says that he knows a thing or two about airplanes. Even though he's crazy, he's their only chance.

Will Matt and Two Moons ever get to soar above the clouds, or will their flying be limited to their dreams?

—*Cynthia Cordes*
Onondaga County Public Library, Syracuse, NY

📖 Blue Heron

Avi. Bradbury, 1992. 185p. Hardbound (ISBN 0-02-707751-9) $14.95. **Grades 5–8 . 4Q, 4P (M. A. Capan); Grades 7-12. 3Q, 2P (P. Jones).**

"What's that?" Maggie asked her father late one fall afternoon, as they stood near the shore of the Massachusetts lake near their home.

"A blue heron," he said. Maggie watched in awe as the magnificent bird flew from the nearby marsh out over the water. Lying in bed later that night, Maggie remembered the beautiful and mysterious blue-gray bird. Thinking of it made her sad, although she didn't know why.

The next morning, Maggie got up early and walked through the morning mist to the edge of the marsh. Deep in thought, she didn't notice the heron until she was very close to it. Four feet tall, it stood on two spindly, fragile-looking legs. Its back and wings were covered with blue-gray feathers, and its white head was topped with striped black feathers that made a crown-like plume. The heron's beak was pointed and dagger-like, and its eyes were the color of lemons. It looked strange and magical.

Every morning Maggie went to the large flat rock beside the marsh to watch the heron, and to protect it from the boy who wanted to kill it just for fun. Gradually the blue heron became Maggie's lifeline, her support and her friend, a way to deal with the problems Maggie had to face every day. But can even the power of the heron help her when the problem she faced was death?

—*Mary Ann Capan*
Western Illinois University, Macomb, IL

M aggie clutches the crystal in her hand as her plane lands. Maggie believes in magic. She used to believe that magic was used to change things, but now she thinks that magic is for keeping things the same. Maggie clutches the crystal and wishes everything could be as it was before. Before her parents divorced, before her father moved away, before he remarried, before he and his new wife had another child, before she only saw her father during these twice-a-year trips. Because everything changes.

Maggie clutches the crystal as Joanna, her father's new wife, drives her to the cottage where she will be staying with them this summer. The cottage is on a lake, and that's where Maggie sees the blue heron for the first time. The heron, so beautiful, so perfect, so magical. Her father tells her that the blue heron is a symbol for either life or death, and that she must choose between them because everything changes. Maggie clutches the crystal as she sneaks out each morning to watch the blue heron. Putting her alarm clock under her pillow, she wakes up before anyone else to go down to the lake to watch the heron, and maybe one day, even get to touch it. All is peaceful and all is quiet, but the morning she finds a bow and arrow, Maggie realizes all that will change. She is sure someone is trying to kill the blue heron. Life and death, and everything changes.

And things about Maggie's father are changing. He isn't the person she's known all her life. There are the mysterious phone calls that seem so important and so intense. There are the bursts of rage that come from nowhere, and the way he talks to Maggie and Joanna. There is the bottle of pills he refuses to take, the secrets he refuses to share, and the way he talks about death. For Maggie's father, everything has already changed.

Maggie clutches the crystal and remembers what her father said about the heron being a symbol for life or death. But the heron is being hunted by a boy who wants to kill it for fun, and her father is being hunted by thoughts he won't share with anyone, and Maggie doesn't know whether it is she or the heron who is to make the choice between life and death. Will she have a chance to save both her father and the heron?

—*Patrick Jones*
Allen County Public Library, Fort Wayne, IN

Blue River

Ethan Canin. Houghton Mifflin, 1991. 222p.
Hardbound (ISBN 0-395-49854-6) $19.95.
Adults. 4Q, 2P.

T here were two kinds of people in the world, his brother Lawrence had told him: those who wanted to be killed and those who did the killing. Edward had idolized Lawrence as a child, and even as an adult, just the mention of his brother's name was enough to make Edward remember Lawrence's power over him.

Lawrence was always in trouble, living on the edge. But he had a way with women and a way with words that managed to get him out of trouble most of the time. Edward, on the other hand, lived life cautiously, always playing it safe, although Lawrence had had an enormous influence on him. In fact, Edward knew he was probably an ophthalmologist today because Lawrence taught him to observe the world scientifically.

It wasn't surprising that two brothers so different would drift apart. They hadn't seen each other more than a couple of times in 15 years when Lawrence showed up again, running from trouble and wanting to be a part of Edward's life again. But Edward was uncomfortable with Lawrence in the house and felt protective of his wife and son. Lawrence could not stay. He *must* not stay. Edward gave his brother clean clothes and some money and drove him to the bus station. But when the bus pulled out of the station, Edward was compelled to follow it down the road. He had to be sure that Lawrence was on the bus, that he hadn't sneaked off. It had happened once before, back in Blue River, and as Edward followed the bus, the memories of his childhood began to flood his mind. It was time to face the truth about Lawrence and about himself. It could be avoided and ignored no longer.

—*Maureen Whalen*
Rochester Public Library, Rochester, NY

The Borning Room

Paul Fleischman. HarperCollins, 1991. 101p.
Hardbound (ISBN 0-06-023785-6) $13.95.
Grades 6–12, 4Q, 2P.

It is the year of our Lord nineteen hundred and eighteen. The war against the Kaiser is raging in Europe. Here in Ohio, the snow falls in the January twilight. My name is Georgina Caroline Lott Bock, and I am 67 years old. Like so many others of my family before me, I lie here in bed in what we call the borning room. It is the room where women in my family come to give birth to their children, where they nurse those children when they are ill, and where they feel the joy of their recovery or the pain of their death. It is the room where the tired bodies of our family members come to die, just as I have done. But I do not fear death, for I have had a rich and full life.

I was born in this room, and when I was eight, I sat beside my mother and held her hand while my brother Zeb was born. When I was 12, I held my grandfather's hand as he died, remembering how he had taught me to respect nature and value life. I talked to him for hours, hoping that somehow the sound of my voice would keep him alive. But I dozed off, and he died. When I awoke and reached for his hand, it was still and cold, and as I realized that he was dead, the stories he had told me began to come back to me.

So take my hand and come with me now to the borning room, and I will share its stories with you.

—*Joanne Foss*
Lancaster County Public Library, Lancaster, PA

The Brave

Robert Lipsyte. HarperCollins, 1991. 195p. Hardbound (ISBN 0-06-023915-8) $14.95. **Grades 7–12. 4Q, 4P.**

All Sonny really wanted to do was join the Army. He'd traveled all the way from the reservation to New York City to get his mom to sign the papers so he could enlist. But before that could happen, Sonny's personal monster—his raging, uncontrollable temper that ruined his concentration in the boxing ring—started him down the road to self-destruction.

The city was called "The Big Apple," but when Sonny reached for it, he reached in the wrong direction. Growing up on the reservation, he was too lonely and too naive to be able to recognize the sharks that roamed the streets looking for innocents to prey on. Stick and Doll said they were his friends, but that didn't mean much when it came from a drug dealer and a prostitute looking for an easy mark. It wasn't long before he landed in jail for defending Doll and nailing a police officer with his wicked left hook. Uncle Jake had raised Sonny as the last of the Running Braves. Now he needed every bit of the courage that had given him to go on.

He could see only one chance, a chance offered by a detective named Alfred Brooks, who was different from most of the cops Sonny'd met. Brooks thought Sonny had what it took to be a championship boxer, and was willing to work with him to make that happen—IF. Sonny's temper, his monster, was in the way. He seemed out of control—and winning meant control. It was impossible to win without it. Sonny had a great knockout punch, but without control it wasn't enough to make him a champion.

Will Sonny's monster reach out and grab him again, and help the Big Apple swallow him whole, or will he be able to turn that monster into the hawk that Uncle Jake had

said was waiting to be set free? Champion or failure. . . which way will he go?

—*Bernice D. Crouse*
Fulton County Library, McConnellsburg, PA

Breaking the Ring

Donna Walsh Inglehart. Little, Brown, 1991. 148p. Hardbound (ISBN 0-316-41867-6) $13.95. **Grades 7–8. 3Q, 3P.**

The River. Jessie can't wait for summer to begin so she can get back to her grandparents' summer cottage on the St. Lawrence River. It's been six years since she was there, and she's sure that this summer will be just as wonderful and exciting as all the ones she remembers were. And at first, it seemed like she was right. Exploring, shopping, and getting reacquainted with the river and the town on its banks are just part of what Jessie, her best friend Maggie, and her sister Emma spend their days doing. Jessie goes sailing with Jeff, another summer resident. Maggie parties with a group of college kids, and they're both sure that nothing could possibly spoil their summer.

But that all changes the day they decide to explore Maple Island. It's supposed to be haunted by a hermit who was killed there, but what they discover is far more frightening than any ghost could be. The cache of drugs they find suddenly makes their summer far more exciting and dangerous than they'd really wanted it to be. Their Fourth of July celebration ends in a high-speed boat chase to a castle, complete with dungeons and full of criminals who would just love to make sure that Jessie and Maggie never escape from them. Will the two be able to survive *Breaking the Ring*, or will those dungeon cells have permanent occupants once again?

—*Patsy Launspach*
Indian Ridge Middle School, El Paso, TX

Catalyst

Philip Cornford. Bantam, 1991. 425p. Hardbound (ISBN 0-553-07122-X) $19.50. **Adults. 4Q, 3P.**

Get out your passport and strap on your bulletproof vest—you're going on a worldwide trip with danger waiting at the touch of a button. Terrorist bombs are set to go off all over Europe if their makers get the wrong answer. Bush and Gorbachev may have been promoting world peace and understanding, but this story shows the discontent and distrust that were lurking just under the surface.

The embarrassed world leaders know that they have to catch the terrorists and destroy the bombs before the bombs destroy most of Europe. But how do you trace a team of mad bombers who blow up themselves along with their targets? Bannon, the best of the CIA, and Klimenti, the best of the KGB, are put on the case. Two men trained not to trust each other must now work together. It may be the new world order, but how effective will this team of strange bedfellows really be? Will they own up when TV reporters ask if they're making progress? Are they ready to do the detail work that can make or break this case? And most importantly, can they learn to trust each other enough to share their individual discoveries and begin to put the pieces of the puzzle together in a way that makes sense?

Follow along with Bannon and Klimenti as they struggle to work against their enemy and not against each other.

—Mark Anderson
Fairfax County Public Library, Fairfax, VA

The Chemo Kid

Robert Lipsyte. HarperCollins, 1992. 167p. Hardbound (ISBN 0-06-02024-X) $14.00. **Grades 7–12. 3Q, 3P.**

You know what they'll write about Fred in the yearbook? "He was here. We think."

Fred was the kind of guy who stayed out of trouble because no one even knew he was around. That could have its benefits when Fred caught the two heavies of the school, Tank the linebacker and Roger the dope dealer—who was also the mayor's nephew—in the bathroom on prom night, shooting up steroids. Cool—NOT.

Fred's most memorable words were: "Most people are just empty Styrofoam burger boxes floating along the storm drains of life, but the hero is a person with a cold fire."

Fred the Styrofoam box threatened to be trashed, not only because of those stupid lumps Tank and Roger, but also because of another stupid lump: cancer. And fat chance that Styrofoam Fred would metamorphose into a cold-fire hero.

The only time Fred was a hero was when he was the GameMaster, when he played Ranger. Like Fred, Ranger sort of floated in and out. Unlike Fred, Ranger was a wandering hero: "Protect the Needy. Always choose Right over Wrong." Only one problem: Ranger always died.

Now it looked like the other thing Styrofoam-box Fred would have in common with cold-fire Ranger was death, one way or another. That is, until he became the Chemo Kid.

—Lesley Farmer
San Domenico School, San Anselmo, CA

The Christie Caper

Carolyn G. Hart. Bantam, 1991. 317p. Hardbound (ISBN 0-553-07404-0) $18.00. **Adults. 4Q, 3P.**

Glass shattered and shards of the Death on Demand Bookstore's front window crashed to the floor. Customers ran for cover, but Annie Darling, the shop's owner, ran to the front of the store. "Oh my God," she said to herself, "Gunfire . . . at my store." The south front window lay in twinkling pieces on the bookstore floor. It was not the way she'd expected to begin the highly celebrated week-long Agatha Christie Convention, in honor of the mystery writer's hundredth birthday.

Annie could hear Neil Bledsoe cursing as he bullishly shoved his way back into the shop. She had just more or less thrown him out. He was a literary critic—rude, obnoxious, tactless, cruel, and bordering on evil. He'd made a career of making everyone's lives miserable and was threatening to ruin Annie's well-planned and internationally recognized convention. Could it be that he'd finally insulted the wrong person for the last time? Without a doubt, the shots had been meant for Neil as he left the store. A cold chill swept over Annie. Her thoughts turned dark and apprehensive. Her close friend Emma Clyde had come painfully close to running down Neil just a few days ago. But Annie had to admit that Emma was far from the only person who hated Neil. Her book was just one of the many he'd torn to pieces in his reviews.

But a murder attempt at the Christie convention? It seemed like an ironic and powerful practical joke—or was it? A joke played out in real life, in absolute reality . . . . A part of the celebration of Dame Christie's legacy—or cold-blooded revenge?

—Nancy Fritz Bunnell
Knox County Career Center, Mount Vernon, OH

David and Jonathan

Cynthia Voight. Scholastic, 1992. 256p. Hardbound (ISBN 0-590-45165-0) $14.95. **Grades 9–12, adults. 4Q, 3P.**

Until David came, the war was just a game to Henry and Jonathan, something very far away, something that wouldn't be important until they were adults. Even though Jonathan knew some of his relatives had been killed by the Nazis, the war in Korea was more real in 1952 than World War II. David changed all that.

David was Jonathan's cousin. He was in the Nazis' concentration camps and survived, but he almost didn't survive the displaced-person camps where he'd lived since the war. He didn't want to eat or sleep, and he let no one get to know him. The doctors in the camps decided that he would do better if he were part of a family, so he came to live with Jonathan's family. And for Jonathan and Henry, nothing was ever the same again.

Even though he was 20 years old, David went to high school with Henry and Jonathan. When Jonathan went over to Henry's after school, David went too. Henry couldn't understand David—it seemed like he was competing with Henry over every little thing, even over Jonathan's friendship. And Jonathan wasn't any fun any longer. It was more than the fact that he didn't laugh or play anymore; it was even more than David's constant presence with him. It was something about the way he watched David, as if maybe he was going to dry up and disappear. Henry couldn't figure it out, and it drove him nuts—until the day that David disappeared.

—*Marijo Duncan*
Phoenix Public Library, Phoenix, AZ

Dear One

Jacqueline Woodson. Delacorte, 1991. 145p. Hardbound (ISBN 0-385-30416-1) $14.00. **Grades 7–12. 4Q, 3P.** Reviewed in: Bklst, 11/15/91, p. 619; SLJ, 6/91, p. 129.

"I don't want a pregnant girl in my house!" Feni screamed at her mother. She was furious, really furious. Her mother had decided that Rebecca should come and live with them until after her baby was born. She'd been having problems at home ever since she told her family she was pregnant. Because her mother and Feni's mother were friends, they decided it would be best for Rebecca to get away from Harlem and live with Feni and her mother.

Feni hadn't had much experience with Harlem or with pregnant girls. She went to a private school, where none of the girls dared show up pregnant. But when Rebecca showed up at Feni's front door, she was definitely pregnant, and definitely *not* the kind of person who fitted into Feni's world. To begin with, she had a chip on her shoulder about almost everything, and Feni decided right away that Rebecca was the rudest girl she'd ever met.

If someone had told Feni when she first met Rebecca that they would get to be friends, she would've laughed in their face. It took awhile for her to see through Rebecca's

attitude to the scared person inside, and to discover that there's more to having a baby than being pregnant.

—*Marijo Duncan*
Phoenix Public Library, Phoenix, AZ

Do or Die

Leon Bing. Nonfiction. HarperCollins, 1991. 277p. Hardcover (ISBN 0-06-016326-7) $19.95. **Grades 9–12, adults. 3Q, 3P.**

Some of the kids you'll meet in this book are homeless, but most have some kind of a home, even if it's with only one parent or guardian, who might be a crackhead, willing to do almost anything for money. You'll meet G-Roc, Li'l Monster, Silencer, Hooks, Wimpy, Bopete, Sniper, Monster Kody, and others. They live in Los Angeles. They are members of the Crips and the Bloods gangs. This is their story.

G-Roc, or Gangster-Roc, is 15. He is one of the rare members of the Crips who has two working and caring parents at home, yet he's been a Crip since he was eight. For G-Roc, being a Crip includes car-jacks, stealing, selling drugs, and drive-by shootings. He calls it "working for the hood"—his neighborhood gang. He wants to have a bad rep so he can fulfill his gang name—be a criminal, be devious, do anything, be bad to the fullest—fight, shoot, kill, whatever.

Monster Kody, 29, is a success. He's fulfilled his gang name so well that everybody either wants him dead or wants to be just like him. Monster Kody is what all gang members, Bloods and Crips alike, call a "movie star," or an "O.G."—original gangster—the top of the line.

He's been ambushed and shot six times at close range because he had an awesome rep and was an O.G. at 17. As a star, he put in more work for the hood than anyone else. He did the dirty work that no one else would do, going into houses where no one else would go, shooting people, walking into enemy territory where no one else would go—suicide missions. Even today, he's still considered to be a star, courageous, daring, but now he knows he was just plain stupid.

Monster Kody educated himself during the years he spent in prison. Today, at 29, he's married and still living in and fighting for the hood he grew up in. And though he's still considered to be a Crip, he's a Crip with a mission. He tells the boys of the hood that he's a success story because he's a "ghetto intellectual," and that getting an education is the only way to learn to be yourself and not be a criminal, to be proud of yourself and your heritage, to stand straight and walk tall. Monster Kody knows that education is the only thing that will help his hood survive, that will ensure that he will live to see his own kids grow up.

You've read about the Crips and the Bloods in the newspapers, you've heard about them on TV, and you know about their battles and their reputations. Now get to know the people behind those stories. These are the individuals behind the names in the headlines, the gang members who fight for their hoods, knowing that they must always be ready to do or die.

—*Faye A. Powell*
Prince George's County Memorial Library System,
District Heights, MD

Don't Be S.A.D.: A Teenage Guide to Handling Stress, Anxiety, and Depression

Susan Newman. Photographs by George Tiboni. Nonfiction. Julian Messner, 1992. 121p. Paperbound (ISBN 0-671-72611-0) $8.95. 121p. Hardbound (ISBN 0-671-72610-2) $12.98. **Grades 7–12. 3Q, 1P.**

What would you do if you were Cindy, with her schedule? She's a high school junior, and her day begins at 5:30 a.m. School starts at 7:20 and is over at 2:15. After school she has band practice and two nights a week, swim practice. On choir nights she doesn't get home till about 9:30, and then she still has tons of homework to do. She's also in student government, the Art Club, the school musical, and on the Homecoming Court.

Sounds pretty good to you? If I were a teenager, I think it would sound like a dream come true—but is it really? Cindy's always so tired from being on the go, on stage, that she doesn't really enjoy much of it anymore. Even being on the Homecoming Court just means having to smile all the time to get votes. But she feels like she can't quit anything, because so many people are depending on her. Her life is getting more and more crazy, and it seems like there's no way out.

But Cindy is only one of the people you'll meet in this book who can show you that there is a way out—a way out of stress, a way out of anxiety, a way out of depression. Your life doesn't have to be out of control. Find out what Cindy and Jackie and Peter and others did, and you may discover some answers for your own life. You don't have to be stressed, anxious, or depressed.

—*Sharon Thomas*
Goddard Intermediate/Junior High Library, Goddard, KS

Dope and Trouble

Elliot Currie. Nonfiction. Pantheon Books, 1992. 290p. Hardbound (ISBN 0-394-96151-1) $ 22.00. **Grades 9–12, adults. 3Q, 2P.**

I want you to meet Blaster, Spooky, Lucifer, Cindi, Rocket Queen, Teresa, Loca, Virginia, and James L. They're teenagers with something to tell you about what they think and how they live. These teens are drug dealers and users, gang members, thieves, and more. They come from all kinds of backgrounds: ghettos in the city, wealthy suburban neighborhoods, black, white, Hispanic. And each of them can tell you about some of the harsh realities of their lives.

Blaster talks about his life as a dealer. "It's dangerous to walk outside, [but] you gonna die young or you gonna die old, simple as that." Rocket Queen isn't so casual about the thought of death. "I don't want to die, but I think I going to." Teresa first used PCP when she was nine, and tells about one time she was so strung out she "couldn't eat, 'cause the food was moving." Loca admits what her problem is: "I like violence—that's my problem." And sometimes Virginia, who's only 14, wishes and hopes for the future: "Maybe one of these days I'll come back to be a real person."

Come meet these 20 teens, and listen to their stories with an open heart and mind. They're telling it to you straight, letting you in on what they learned by living with dope, and how they discovered that dope and trouble *always* go together.

—*Faye A. Powell*
Prince George's County Memorial Library System,
District Heights, MD

Dracula Unbound

Brian Aldiss. HarperCollins, 1991. 196p. Hardbound (ISBN 0-06-016593-6) $18.95. **Grades 9–12, adults. 3Q, 3P.**

Almost everyone has heard of vampires. Some people even say they believe that vampires really exist, although there's never been any real proof. And no one seems to be able to really agree on what vampires are like—do they abhor garlic, or laugh at someone who uses it as protection? If they go out during the day, do they get sunburned—or burned up entirely? What if they used sun block—would that help? And what if someone found absolute proof, proof that couldn't have been faked, that vampires really did exist in the past, and perhaps do exist in the present and future?

That's exactly what happened at an archaeological dig in a barren Utah desert. Two wooden coffins are discovered in the layer of earth beneath a dinosaur grave. They contain two bodies. In one of them is a silver bullet; in the other, a wooden stake. Vampires and dinosaurs co-existed on Earth? But that's only one bizarre discovery. There's also a ghost train that rumbles through the camp every night. On board the terror train are Joe Bodenland, inventor of the time manipulator, and Bram Stoker, author of *Dracula*. They are investigating the discovery at the camp, searching not only for evidence of vampires in the Paleozoic past but also for a possible nuclear apocalypse set up for the future by hordes of the Undead.

—*Jeff Blair*
Olathe South High School, Olathe, KS

The Dragon of Middlethorpe

Anne Leo Ellis. Holt, 1991. 180p. Hardbound (ISBN 0-8050-1713-5) $14.95. **Grades 5–8. 3Q, 3P.**

The dragon is back! Kate has always wanted to see the dragon, even though the last time it appeared her grandfather led nine men into the forest to hunt for it—none of whom was ever seen again. But now, listening to the rumors of poisoned waters, shadows flying overhead, and tongues of fire in the sky, Kate is almost as frightened as everyone else.

However, in spite of her fear, when Kate learns that her father, Master Simon, is going to lead the villagers on a dragon hunt, she's determined to go along. She knows that a girl, a mere maid, would never be allowed to go on a hunt, so she disguises herself in her brother's clothes. But before the hunt leaves the village, her mother discovers what Kate has done. She not only doesn't get to go on the hunt, she also has to listen to the hunters' jeers and laughter as they leave. The humiliation is almost more than she can bear.

But Kate is not a typical maid of the Middle Ages, and she is determined to get at least a glimpse of the dragon. She decides that the hunters may need the magical healing qualities of powdered unicorn horn, and sets off alone into the forest to take it to them. "Who knows what will happen," she thinks to herself. "Maybe I'll be lucky enough to see the dragon after all."

—*Diane Deuel*
Central Rappahannock Regional Library, Fredericksburg, VA

Dragon War

Laurence Yep. HarperCollins, 1992. 313p. Hardcover (ISBN 0-06-020302-1) $15.00. **Grades 5–8. 3Q, 2P.** Reviewed in: SLJ, 6/92, p. 144; PW, 5/18/92, p. 71; Bklst, 4/15/92, p. 1524.

The purple and orange sea worms slithered into General Winter's armor. The General froze as one worm (maybe poisonous?) wriggled up his chest and raised its head to stare at his face. General Winter began to scream, sounding remarkably like a teakettle.

Monkey grinned. It was good to have something to grin about. The war had been long and hard. Shimmer, princess of the dragons, and Monkey's friend, lay unconscious, perhaps dying. Thorn, another friend, had given his soul to help Shimmer in her battle against the Boneless King. But he and Shimmer might yet be saved if Monkey and the dragon people could just drive the Boneless King from the dragons' lands. It looked hopeless—the King had Thorn's soul and great magic to help him.

But Monkey still grinned. (It's hard to get Monkey down.) After all, anyone who could escape from a sealed mountain, pull hairs from his tail and turn them into tiny monkeys, somersault endlessly through the air, and live underwater could easily defeat the evil Boneless King!

But if Monkey had known what lay ahead, maybe that grin would have faded. The Boneless King was far from defeated, Thorn was still gone, and Shimmer was still very sick, if not dying. Would Monkey be able to win the war without the help of his friends?

—*Julie Bray*
Jasper County Public Library, Rensselaer, IN

[This is the fourth book in the Dragon series by Yep. The first ones are *Dragon of the Lost Sea*, *Dragon Steel*, and *Dragon Cauldron*.—**Ed.**]

The Drowning of Stephan Jones

Bette Greene. Bantam, 1991. 217p. Hardbound (ISBN 0-553-07437-7) $16.00. **Grades 9–12, adults. 2Q, 3P.**

They had been so careful. They had both been tested for AIDS, and besides, there had been no one else for Stephan but Frank for five years. They were more than business partners. They had made a lifelong commitment to each other. All they wanted was a peaceful place to enjoy the success of their antiques business and, more important, each other.

Parsons Springs, Arkansas, held promise for them, the promise of a home and happiness. It was a tourist town crammed with an intriguing mix of little shops and restaurants, with an eclectic population as varied as its storefronts. Stephan was sure that here he and Frank would be accepted. Better than Boston. Better than the seminary.

But that was before the terror began. The promise of peace shriveled and fear took its place. First there were hate-filled stares, then ugly words like "pervert" and "sinner." Frank shrugged them off, but Stephan couldn't. And when the harassment began in earnest, even Frank couldn't ignore the physical abuse and vitriolic letters written by a boy whose bigotry seemed to be shared by everyone in the neighboring community of Rachetville.

And when the hatred and bigotry finally peaked, that same boy stood looking into the wild water of the Pascaloosa River waiting to see where Stephan would rise to the surface. Would he come up right where they'd thrown him in, or would he try to sneak away by swimming downstream a little? He didn't want to miss seeing where he came up—he and his friends had plans for Stephan. They'd show him what happened to queers in Rachetville—just as soon as he came up, they'd *really* show him.

—*Nancy Chu*
Western Illinois University, Macomb, IL

E, My Name Is Emily

Norma Fox Mazer. Scholastic, 1991. 167p.
Hardcover (ISBN 0-590-43653-8) $13.95.
Grades 5–8. 3Q, 3P.
Reviewed in: SLJ, 11/91, p. 120.

More than anything else, Emily wants her mother and father to get back together again so they can all live together as a family, just like they did before the divorce. Since the divorce, it seems like Emily's life has been falling apart—everything is going wrong!

Her mother is dating their landlord, weird Mr. Linaberry. Emily can't figure out what her mother sees in him. It doesn't matter to Emily that he can fix leaky faucets, the hole in the screen, or all the other little things that constantly need fixing. It doesn't matter that he always seems to be around to help them just when they need it most. To Emily, the only thing that matters is that it's unnatural for her mother to be dating anyone, especially someone as ugly as Mr. Linaberry.

And Emily has her own problems with romance, too. Robertson Reo is positive that Emily is his true love, even though he's younger than she is. He's determined to make her like him—and Emily isn't at all sure what she wants to do about it.

To top things off, Emily is fighting with her best friend, Bunny. It seems that all of a sudden Bunny thinks that Robertson is awfully cute and a good kisser besides! Emily isn't even sure why she's mad at Bunny; she doesn't even like Robertson—or does she?

Find out how Emily and her mother figure out what to do about their lives and their romances.

—*Paulette Nelson*
Minot Public Library, Minot, ND

Earth to Matthew

Paula Danziger. Delacorte, 1991. 148p. Hardcover (ISBN 0-385-30453-6) $14.00. **Grades 5–8. 3Q, 3P.**

Hi, I'm Matthew, and my life is pretty complicated right now. Let me tell you about it. We're talking about the environment in school right now, particularly ecosystems. It's really getting complicated. Science used to be easier to understand.

For instance, the other day, when our teacher asked for an example of how one thing environmentally affects something else, my nemesis Vanessa blurts out (she's always blurting out something!): "Like if someone, who will remain nameless, was absent from school, that would make me very happy." Jerk. I call out, "Like if someone, who will remain nameless, was outside and a giant vulture swooped down and captured her and the babies ate her and then they barfed and fell out of their nest into the water and polluted the water and the fish who got sick got scooped up and sold to the company that sells stuff to the school cafeteria and we all got sick. That's how it works, right?"

The teacher wasn't impressed. All she said was, "No name calling." Hey, nobody was using names, right?

But there's something else to be said about ecosystems. My sister, for instance, is really getting our whole family out of balance, eco-wise. She's gotten pretty strange lately—that is, if you call wearing all black and getting your head shaved pretty strange. I don't know . . . . Maybe it would be better to be a rain forest—at least then someone would pay attention to me.

I guess it all just gets to me. That's why right now it's *Earth to Matthew.*

—*Lesley Farmer*
San Domenico School, San Anselmo, CA

Eleven Kids, One Summer

Ann M. Martin. Holiday House, 1991. 152p.
Hardcover (ISBN 0-8234-0912-0) $13.95.
Grades 3–6. 3Q, 3P.

Meet the Rosso family: Abigail, 15; Bainbridge, 14; Calandra, 13; Dagwood, 12; Eberhard, 11; the twins, Faustine and Gardenia, 10; Hannah, 9; Ira, 8; Janthina, 7; and Keegan, 6 months. And that's just the kids! There's also Mr. and Mrs. Rosso, and the family cat, Zsa-Zsa.

Nothing is easy with eleven kids and one cat, but nothing is ever dull, boring, or lonely. This summer promises to be no different. The whole family is going to spend the entire summer on Fire Island. Just the trip there is quite an adventure—there's three train changes and a ferry crossing, all of which pose problems when it's necessary to keep track of 13 people, one cat, and all their luggage. But the trip is only the first adventure. Many more are waiting for each of the Rossos when they finally get to their summer home on Fire Island.

—*Cynthia L. Lopuszynski*
Lafayette, IN

📖 Ellie Brader Hates Mr. G

Janet Johnston. Clarion, 1991. 131p. Hardbound (ISBN 0-395-58195-8) $13.95. **Grades
3–6. 3Q, 3P.**

Have you ever had a teacher you really liked? I mean,
really, *really* liked? I did. My name is Ellie Brader,
and Ms. Simpson, who was our teacher when I started fifth
grade, was my very favorite. School was great until we
started having substitutes. We had a different sub every day
for a week, which was bad enough, but then we got the
really bad news. Ms. Simpson wasn't coming back, because her mother was very sick and Ms. Simpson had to
help take care of her.

Our teacher for the rest of the year was Mr. Garrett.
He was old—*very* old. He'd already retired, he was so old,
until they asked him to come back to teach our class. I knew
I wasn't going to like him, especially when he started
changing all Ms. Simpson's rules. He said, "No more line
leaders. You're almost in the sixth grade now." He was lots
more strict about homework, too—"No homework, no
recess." But the biggest change was about Bingo, our pet
rabbit. You see, at the end of the school year, there was
going to be a drawing to see who got to keep Bingo over
the summer. Ms. Simpson had said only people with Bs or
better got to be part of the drawing. Mr. Garrett said anyone
who brought a note from home could be part of the drawing.
When we asked him why, he just said, "I don't reward good
conduct, I expect it." I knew I'd *never* win Bingo.

But even if I hated Mr. G., everything was going okay
until something horrible happened. Bingo died. He died
while I was taking care of him over the weekend. I felt
awful, but I knew it wasn't my fault. He just died. Everyone
in class was upset and some of them even said *I* killed him!
That's why I couldn't believe what Mr. G. did about it. I'll
never figure teachers out—never!

—**Cynthia L. Lopuszynski**
Lafayette, IN

📖 Everybody's Daughter

Marsha Qualey. Houghton Mifflin, 1991.
201p. Hardbound (ISBN 0-395-55870-0)
$13.95. **Grades 7– 12. 3Q, 2P.**

Just once I wish someone could *not* want something from
me! Teachers want good grades and proper behavior.
My parents want me to obey their rules—in fact, they just
assume I will! Girlfriends want the juicy details of my
personal life, and my boyfriend Andy wants me to have sex
with him. Martin, our neighbor, wants . . . just what *does*
Martin want?

It all started 18 years ago when a group of college
students, including my parents, began a commune here in
Minnesota. They lived, worked, and played together for 10
years. Even after they disbanded, the commune members
couldn't really leave my parents behind. They still want
their advice, their money, and a place at the wood stove in
our house. They still think of me as the first baby born in
their commune. I feel smothered—crowded by all the
people around me. I feel like I'm losing control of my life.
There's a huge void between my life with my family and
friends and my life the way I'd like it to be. I wish a
magician would come along and wave a magic wand and
change it or make them all just go away. Then I wouldn't
have to be *Everybody's Daughter*.

—**Mary Ann Capan**
Western Illinois University, Macomb, IL

📖 Fat Glenda Turns Fourteen

Lila Perl. Clarion, 1991. 168p. Hardbound
(ISBN 0-395-53341-4) $13.95. **Grades 5–8.
3Q, 4P.**

You can use lots of words to describe someone who
weighs too much—*large, plump, heavy, stout,
chubby, chunky, big,* and just plain *fat*. Glenda has heard
them all, and right now she feels like they all describe her
perfectly. She's gained 11 pounds, and she's positive that's
why Justin hasn't written to her since they met last summer.
Somehow he must know she's gained weight! What other
reason could he possibly have for not writing?

Glenda is 14, fat, and miserable. Even her best
friends, Mary Lou and Patty, can't cheer her up. But
everything changes when Giselle moves to town. Next to
Giselle, Glenda looks positively thin! Giselle isn't just fat,
she's huge, even obese. But she doesn't let her size get in
her way—in fact, she used to be a model (for plus sizes, of
course), and she thinks Glenda is just the type the All-Girl
Modeling Agency is looking for.

Glenda can't believe it—from fat to fashion model in
one easy step! She uses Giselle's tips on her hair, makeup,
dress, and posture, and starts her new career. Her biggest
assignment is a runway fashion show. She worries about
falling down or missing one of her cues, but what really
happens to her that day is more bizarre than anything she's
ever imagined.

—**Lisa Broadhead**
Bartow Public Library, Bartow, FL

📖 Finn's Island

Eileen Dunlop. Holiday House, 1991. 128p.
Hardbound (ISBN 0-8234-0910-4) $13.95.
Grades 5–8. 4Q, 3P.

Long ago, when he was a boy, my grandfather carried
these things from Hirsay Island. [Show the audience
a small box or tin, preferably battered or old, and take out

of it a white feather, a smooth black stone, a snippet of gray wool, a snail shell, and a yellowed envelope.]

These things, and his memories, were all he took when he left his childhood home. One thing in this box has the potential to heal thousands of people of a painful disease—but that's the end of my story.

I don't really remember the beginning of my story, because it started when I first heard Grandpa talk about Hirsay Island, and he's been telling me about it for as long as I can remember. He made it seem like a wonderful, almost magical place: wild, remote, with cozy cottages, hardworking fishermen, laughing children climbing the cliffs, pretty star-shaped flowers growing everywhere. How I longed to go there! When our boarder, Douglas Cooper, invited me to join him on an expedition to the island, I was the happiest boy in the world. But that happiness soured when I discovered that Doug's son Chris would be going too. I didn't want to share Hirsay with anyone, especially not Chris, who'd already climbed mountains, sailed the seas, and cycled back-country roads. But I didn't have a choice—if I were to go to Hirsay, it would be with Chris.

As it turned out, nothing was what I had expected— not the island and not Chris. At first, I was bitterly disappointed in my grandfather for telling me such romantic tales about Hirsay, and in myself for believing everything he told me. But now, now that I know, I understand.

[Show contents of the box again, as you replace the items in it—the feather, stone, piece of wool, shell. Open the envelope and pour out small black seeds. Poppy seeds would work well, and aren't expensive.] These are the last remaining seeds of the white star-shaped flower the islanders called *pathan*. They aren't easy flowers to get to; in fact, I risked Chris's life trying to pick some. Doug tells me that a medicine can be made from the leaves of the flower, medicine that can heal people in pain. I'm going to plant the seeds and wait. And while I wait, I'm going to remember Hirsay as my Grandpa did . . . .

—*Karol Rockwin*
Longwood School District, Middle Island, NY

[For more information on using props in your booktalks, see Bette Ammon and Gale Sherman's article on this topic on page 57.—**Ed.**]

📖 Flight #116 Is Down

Caroline B. Cooney. Scholastic, 1992. 208p. Hardcover (ISBN 0-590-44465-4) $13.95. **Grades 5–12. 3Q, 3P.**

Sixteen-year-old Heidi Landseth is alone, lonely, and bored at Dove House Estate, just outside the small New York town of Nearing River. She wishes something would happen to break up the monotony of her life.

Seventeen-year-old Patrick Farquhar is a member of the Nearing River Volunteer Ambulance Company and a certified emergency medical technician. He's bored, too, and is just waiting—almost praying—for an emergency, a *real* emergency.

Sixteen-year-old Carly is a runaway who's on her way home again, and wants nothing more than to make up with her twin sister and her parents. She is on Flight 116, flying over rural New York state.

Teenage brothers Daniel and Tucker are still bitter about their parents' divorce a year ago, but are on their way to their father's wedding nevertheless. They are on Flight 116.

Five-year-old Teddie is returning from a trip to visit her grandparents. She has a quarter taped to her hand in case she gets lost and has to call her mother. She is on Flight 116.

All of the people on board Flight 116 expected it to be no different from any other plane flight. But it was. It didn't land at the airport where a crowd of friends and relatives waited to meet its passengers. It crashed near Dove House, and very soon after that Heidi and Patrick were very sorry that they'd been wishing—almost praying—for something to happen.

Heidi, Patrick, Carly, Daniel, Tucker, and Teddie were all strangers until that night, the night that Flight 116 went down.

—*Marvia Boettcher*
Bismarck Public Library, Bismarck, ND

📖 Flying Changes

Lynn Hall. Harcourt Brace Jovanovich, 1991. 148p. Hardbound (ISBN 15-228790-6) $13.95. **Grades 9–12. 3Q, 3P.**

Welcome to adulthood, Denny Browner. I'm not sure why Tyler spent so much time with me the last month. I'd like to believe it was because I blossomed into a gorgeous fox, or because he genuinely liked me. But more likely, it was just because I was handy.

I know Tyler did those things with the rodeo groupies who offered themselves to him on the road, but this was me, giving for the first time ever something I held dear and precious. It meant something to me. Pretty soon, I'll find out what it meant to him.

In the meantime, until he returns—if he returns— from the rodeo circuit, I have to help figure out how we are going to earn a living since Dad had his roping accident. Gram and I can work the saddle shop, but that doesn't bring in much cash. The filly will sell for a big profit, if I can teach her to take lead changes. And Rita says she's coming back to take care of Dad. She's been gone for 10 years. Even if she is my mother, what makes her think we want her back in our lives now?

Please, Tyler, please come back.

—*Karol Rockwin*
Longwood School District, Middle Island, NY

The Fortuneteller in 5B

Jane Breskin Zalben. Holt, 1991. 148p. Hardcover (ISBN 0-8050-1537-X) $14.95. **Grades 5–7. 3Q, 2P.**

"Madame Van Dam. Spiritual Adviser. Have you ever had your fortune told?" the card read. When Allie saw the card, she wondered if this mysterious new neighbor could help her contact her father. Even though he had been dead for a whole year, she still had a hard time grasping the fact that she would never see or talk to him again.

Allie and her friend Jenny were sure that Madame Van Dam was a true witch. After all, she made strange brews with even stranger sounding herbs and spices. She always seemed to know what Allie was feeling and thinking, too. And she had a rabbit named Tabitha! (Who said witches always have to have black cats?)

But what Allie didn't know was that she and Madame Van Dam were connected in a way she'd never dreamed of or imagined, and that her life would change forever, all because of *The Fortuneteller in 5B*.

—*Cara A. Waits*
Tempe Public Library, Tempe, AZ

Freedom Songs

Yvette Moore. Puffin Books, 1992. 168p. Paperbound (ISBN 0-014-036017) $3.99. Orchard, 1991. 168p. Hardbound (ISBN 0-531-05812-3) $14.95. **Grades 7–12, adults. 4Q, 4P.**

In the summer of 1963, when Sheryl (that's just one syllable, like *Shirley* without the *ey*) went to visit her relatives in the south, she had nothing on her mind but learning how to be a "fly girl." She desperately wanted to be a cheerleader with lots of clothes and even more boyfriends. But during the hot months of that summer, Sheryl's world changed as she saw the beginning of the Civil Rights movement, with all of its terrible violence and unbelievable courage. Her Uncle Pete talked to her about voting rights, freedom rides, and sit-ins. And as Sheryl watched and listened, the political climate of America changed, and she changed as well. Sheryl began to realize that she couldn't let others fight against racial injustice for her. It was her

battle just as much as anyone else's, and she decided, in spite of the risk, to do her part.

—*Anna B. Hart*
Fairfax County Public Library, Sherwood Regional Library, Alexandria, VA

The Gift of the Girl Who Couldn't Hear

Susan Shreve. Tambourine, 1991. 79p. Hardbound (ISBN 0-688-10318-9) $12.95. **Grades 5–6. 3Q, 2P.**

"It's no fun being in seventh grade, and no fun being 13," Eliza thinks to herself. She's so busy worrying about how she looks (fat) and how she feels (crabby and miserable) that she never has time to do her homework or study for tests. Her grades have gone from As to Ds, and her friends have gone from 17 to one.

Lucy is the only friend she has left, and Lucy likes everyone. Eliza has known Lucy for 13 years, and Lucy still amazes her. Lucy is totally deaf—she was born that way—but nothing, and I mean nothing, gets her down. Right now she's practicing her singing so she can play an orphan in the school's musical, "Annie," the biggest production of the year. Of course Lucy can't sing at all. She sounds like a foghorn, but because she can't hear herself, she doesn't know.

Now, Eliza *can* sing, and she's been looking forward to singing the lead in the seventh-grade musical for years. But she's too scared she'll fail to even think about trying out. And without that part, there's no way seventh grade can possibly keep from being a total disaster. So how can a gift from Lucy make any difference at all?

—*Marianne Tait Pridemore*
San Jose Public Library, San Jose, CA

Hannah on Her Way

Claudia Mills. Macmillan, 1991. 151p. Hardbound (ISBN 0-02-767011-2) $12.95. **Grades 5–6. 3Q, 3P.**

Who's your best friend? Have you had the same best friend for a lo-o-o-o-ong time? Remember when you first became best friends? Today I want to tell you about Hannah and her brand-new best friend.

Hannah is new at Greenway Park Elementary School, and she's not fitting into fifth grade very well. Oh, she's smart enough, so the homework is no problem, but she hasn't made any friends, and that *is* a problem. Or rather, it's a problem until Caitie moves to town and turns out to be the best friend Hannah has been looking for.

One of the first things Caitie and Hannah do together is get thrown out of art class. Hannah is very artistic, but just how many projects can one person make out of empty bleach bottles? On the way to the principal's office they have a laughing fit, but Mr. Blake doesn't think the situation is nearly as funny as they do.

And that's only the beginning of their adventures. Caitie talks Hannah into cutting off her braid, they write a play to help Samantha with a new boyfriend, and they go to their first boy-girl party and play "Spin the Bottle."

But not everything is wonderful between these two best friends. Caitie wants Hannah to help her cheat on the math final. She knows Hannah will make a good grade, and if Caitie doesn't pass the test, she'll have to stay in fifth grade.

What does being a best friend really mean? Is it right to help a best friend, even when she wants you to break the rules?

—*Susan Trimby*
St. Martin of Tours School, Kankakee, IL

Happy Birthday, Lexie!

Lisa Eisenberg. Viking, 1991. 121p. Hardbound (ISBN 0-670-83553-6) $17.95. **Grades 3–4. 3Q, 3P.**

Finally, Lexie's tenth birthday is only two weeks away! That's just enough time to shop for invitations and plan the best, most unusual birthday party ever. That is, if her parents are ever home long enough to take her shopping!

Then Lexie's mother discovers that Shirley Spitzer is planning to have her birthday party on the very same day as Lexie's, and she's invited all of Lexie's friends! Lexie isn't worried, though. She just tells her mother that because no one likes Shirley anyway, she's sure that everyone will come to her party instead of Shirley's. Lexie's mother doesn't like that idea at all, so she invites Shirley to come over, and tells the two girls to figure out their own solution to the party problem.

Well, now Lexie *has* to talk to Shirley, and she finds out that Shirley isn't as bad as Lexie thought she was. So—they decide to combine their parties. One big party doesn't have to be awful. It could even be fun. In fact, it could turn out to be the biggest, wildest, most unusual birthday party ever!

—*Colleen Smith*
Town of Haldimand Public Library, Caledonia, Ontario, Canada

The Haymeadow

Gary Paulsen. Delacorte, 1992. 195p. Hardbound (ISBN 0-385-30621-0) $15.00. **Grades 5–8. 3Q, 3P.**

Alone. Just 14-year-old me, 2 horses, 4 dogs, and 6,000 sheep. Alone in the haymeadow all summer. Alone with my thoughts. Alone with my memories.

Memories of my great-grandfather: the old man. I look just like him. He was just four-and-a-half years older than I am when he saw this haymeadow. He came over the rise on his horse. Sat on the horse and gazed at the mountains in the distance behind the prairie. Looked north to nothing and south to nothing and said, "This is mine."

Memories of my dad. Dad who was so serious, especially after Mom died. Dad who never had much to say, even when he told me to take care of the sheep for the summer because he had to take care of Tink. True, Tink was our best ranch help and he was dying of cancer. But to make me watch sheep all summer with no advice on how to do it—it was scary.

My first morning with the sheep. Just after I'd spit out the too-bitter breakfast coffee, I heard one of the dogs barking and a sheep bleating and the high-pitched rattle of a snake. I ran for the horses. From now on I'd keep the horses nearby. I rode to the herd and saw the rattler. I picked up a huge rock from the streambed, hoisted it up with both hands, and smashed the snake's head. But saving the lamb? What did I learn in biology about snake bites? I slashed the lamb's leg. There was so much blood, I must have hit an artery. I couldn't save it. I'd lost my first sheep.

When Billy barked, I thought it was another snake, but it was a skunk. When I called Billy, he got even more excited—and so did the skunk. The smell seemed to be smeared all over the dog, all over me, all over the world. The first day wasn't half over yet. What else could go wrong? Too much!

—*Lesley Farmer*
San Domenico School, San Anselmo, CA

Home at Last

David deVries. Dell, 1992. 151p. Paperbound (ISBN 0-440-40621-8) $3.25. **Grades 3–6. 4Q, 4P.**

Billy had been sure that he'd be the only orphan train kid who wouldn't be chosen. Back in New York, the police had given him the choice of living in Randall's Island Almshouse, an orphanage, or going to Nebraska on the orphan train to be adopted by a farm family. And just as he'd expected, he was the only kid left standing on the train platform. But then he heard a man ask, "Your name is Billy? My name is Andersson. Perhaps you'd like to come with me."

Someone had chosen him, but Billy soon discovered that being a part of the Andersson family wasn't going to be easy. Christina Andersson didn't seem too pleased that

Billy had come to live with them. Nils Andersson worked all the time and never smiled. Their son, Oluf, asked Billy lots of questions like "Are you really an orphan?" or "Where'd you come from?" But even though life in Nebraska wasn't what Billy had expected or hoped for, the Anderssons were good to him, and he worked hard for them.

However, no matter how hard he worked, Billy still had plenty of time to get into trouble. Nils caught him smoking in the barn. He stole a deck of cards from the store in town and was caught showing the other kids card tricks. He got into a fight at the church social, and, worst of all, he disobeyed Nils and let Oluf hold the reins of the two big work horses. When the horses were frightened by a loud clap of thunder, they bolted, dragging Oluf with them. He could have been killed if Nils hadn't been able to catch them.

It was after that that Nils said, "You don't deserve a place in this family . . . . You will go back to where you came from." But Billy didn't care—he had a plan that he was certain would work, and nothing and no one was going to stop him.

—*Dorothy Davidson*
Allie Ward Elementary School, Abilene, TX

How to Get Rid of Your Older Brother

Joel L. Schwartz. Dell, 1992. 120p. Paperbound (ISBN 0-440-40623-4) $3.25. **Grades 3–6. 3Q, 4P.**

Who needed an older brother anyway? Jay certainly didn't—particularly when it was an older brother like Louis. Louis, who once suggested that Jay be traded in for a dog. Louis, who began calling Jay Kipper after the dog next door, because their parents refused to make the trade. Louis, who made matters worse by ordering Jay around as though he really were that Irish setter next door. Who needed an older brother like that?

Maybe it wouldn't have been so bad if Louis had ever realized what a terrific young brother he had. Instead, Louis never stopped—he barred Jay from his room and he led the laughter at Jay's problems on the football field. Louis never stopped playing corny jokes on Jay and delighted in finding ways to make him look foolish in front of the whole school. Finally Jay had had enough—he wanted revenge. He set up his master plan, a plan that would stop Louis once and for all. Louis wouldn't know what hit him!

—*Helen Schlichting*
Sac Community School, Sac City, IA

Jayhawker

Patricia Beatty. Morrow, 1991. 224p. Hardbound (ISBN 0-688-09850-9) $13.95. **Grades 3–6. 4Q, 3P.**

Usually night brings sleep and dreams, but sometimes, during the 1800s in rural Kansas, night brought visitors instead. Elijah Tulley was awakened one night to meet a special visitor, a tall man with dark hair and wild gray eyes, whose name was John Brown. The Tulleys soon agreed to help him fight for his cause, freeing the slaves and bringing Kansas into the Union as a free state. They spent many of their nights after that riding to Missouri to free slaves. Lije learned all too quickly that the price of freedom was often very high. His father and his best friend were killed on one of the raids, and Lije was determined to avenge their senseless deaths.

Then Lije was given the chance of a lifetime, a chance to infiltrate the bushwhackers and report back on the activities of Charley Quantrell and his raiders. Could he really live among the very men he'd been fighting and survive? Could he figure out whose cause was just and whose wasn't? Would he ever be able to stop fighting and go back to his family? Ride with Lije and discover what it was like to be a jayhawker.

—*Suzi Smith*
Tulsa City-County Library System, Tulsa, OK

KidStuff: People, Places, and Things to Know

Alice Siegel and Margo McLoone Basta. Illustrated by Ted Enik. Nonfiction. Bantam, 1991. 224p. Paperbound (ISBN 0-553-15914-3) $3.99. **Grades 5–8. 3Q, 2P.**

Have you ever swallowed the secret ingredient 7X?

Should you eat a *samosa* and wear a *kaffiyeh*—or the other way around?

Do you know the name of the stadium in San Diego?

Do you use apple grease on your toast?

How did the cardigan sweater get its name?

What is the significance of the number 76?

Who are the most famous lovers in history?

To find the answers to these questions and to lots of others you're curious about, take a look at *KidStuff*. Amaze all your friends by knowing all the answers, including who has or hasn't had that secret ingredient, 7X!

—*C. Allen Nichols*
Rocky River Public Library, Rocky River, OH

The Kindness of Women

J. G. Ballard. Farrar, Strauss & Giroux, 1992.
343p. Hardbound (ISBN 0-374-18110-1)
$19.95. **Adults. 3Q, 2P.**

Where does a young Britisher fresh out of a Japanese detention camp in Shanghai go? The hero of *Empire of the Sun* continues his adventures in post-World War II China and England—with the kindness of women.

There's his campmate Cleo. Co-conspirators against the Japanese, the two grow like brother and sister. After the war, James leaves Cleo, too full of shared secrets to handle a mature physical relationship with the once-scrawny girl.

There's the Queen of the Night: a black woman's corpse that James uses to explore the mysteries of human anatomy while he's in medical school.

There's also the perky and independent Miriam, who shows him life outside the reach of the scalpel. She brings him equilibrium, family life, and the reality of death.

There's crazy Sally: a flower child of a governess who's a cyclone of novelty. She sends James reeling into a psychedelic maelstrom.

These women are all reflections of James's own obsessions and unresolved childhood conflicts, and they're all healers for his soul.

Experience the kindness of women.

—Lesley Farmer
San Domenico School, San Anselmo, CA

Kiss the Dust

Ellizabeth Laird. Dutton, 1991. 278p. Hardbound (ISBN 0-525-44893-4) $15.00. **Grades 5–12. 4Q, 4P.**

I knew there wasn't a moment to spare. Quickly I bundled up my little sister Hero and the blue floppy-eared rabbit she'd eluded me long enough to snatch up. I skirted around the wall of our garden to the shade of the oleander tree and lifted her over. Mrs. Amina, our neighbor, took in the situation at once as I panted, "We need a taxi right now. They're down at the end of the street in a car. They may be here any minute." My mind went blank when my best friend's mother answered that it would be impossible to get a taxi here at this time of day. What were we going to do?

Mrs. Amina ran to a window and saw the car coming down the road. I raced to the wall once again and there was Daya, my mother, at the back door fussing with all the bags. I yelled at her, "Leave them or they'll get you!" but she was persistent and the bags came over the wall with the samovar, our cooking jar.

You couldn't imagine the fear I felt when I realized that Mrs. Amina intended to drive us to safety in her own car. Helping us escape would expose her and her family to incredible danger. The thought made me numb and silent as the car jerked forward, but I tried to mouth "Goodbye, Leila" to my best friend, who stood at one of the windows watching us drive away.

And this was only the beginning of a flight that led us on a path through the mountains and into two other countries, that took us into exile from our home in Iraq.

You see, I'm a Kurd, and the Iraqi government is slowly eliminating our people. I understood this for the first time months ago. I had gone shopping and saw a young boy shot in the street. My life changed forever in that split second. It happened long ago, but the memory of it is still as vivid and clear as if it had been yesterday.

Would our family ever be together again? My brother Ashanti, who was a rebel fighting for the Kurds; my father, in hiding, who knew he would pay with his life if he were ever found; my mother, near death in a refugee camp; my little sister, who barely remembers life in Iraq. Would our exile ever end?

—Sharon Thomas
Goddard Intermediate/Junior High School Library,
Goddard, KS

Lockie Leonard, Human Torpedo

Tim Winton. Little, Brown, 1991. 148p. Hardbound (ISBN 0-316-94753-9) $13.95. **Grades 7–9. 4Q, 3P.**

Lockie Leonard is thirteen-and-three-quarters years old and truly packin' death! That's surfing lingo, you know, for being free, happy, and totally in control riding the waves. But on land things get complicated, and moving to a new town doesn't help either. Lockie lies low and tries to stay out of trouble—he's not really a trouble sort of guy. But certain people begin to notice him, especially Vicki Streeton, the most popular girl in school. And then all kinds of things begin to happen. Other kids want to hang out with him, he's voted president of the local surfing club, and he realizes he's in love—with Vicki! Vicki, however, isn't so sure about this love thing. It seems love takes time and thought, and digging down deep to find your innermost feelings. It just may be too much for Vicki to take. Can Lockie and Vicki work out this love thing? Will Lockie ever feel like he's "Lucky Lockie" again?

—Ann Liebst
Baker University, Baldwin City, KS

Maria Escapes

Gillian Avery. Illustrated by Scott Snow. Simon & Schuster, 1992. 258p. Hardbound (ISBN 0-671-77074-8) $15.00. **Grades 5–6. 3Q, 2P.**
Reviewed in: SLJ, 6/92, p. 112; PW, 6/8/92, p. 63.

Imagine going to school in a place where everyone is always angry with you and no one wants to be your friend. Imagine having everyone think that you are terribly slow and very untidy. Imagine struggling over an assignment and crying in frustration, so you end up smearing what you had worked so hard to write. Imagine being told that you would have to wear a sign proclaiming your ignorance and untidiness if you didn't redo the assignment correctly. If you were faced with these awful circumstances, what would you do?

For Maria Henniker-Haden, the only solution seems to be running away, and that is what she does. Maria lives in Victorian England in the mid-1800s. She was orphaned when she was very young and lived with an elderly aunt until it was decided she should be sent to school. When she escapes from school, Maria heads for Oxford, where her only other relatives live. Her Uncle Hadden is the warden of Canterbury College, and agrees to allow her to stay with him and be tutored along with the three boys who live next door. But if Maria thinks that learning will be any easier here than it was at school, she's in for a shock, and for lots of adventures with the boys and their tutor.

—*Terrie Ratcliffe*
Irving Public Library, Irving, TX

Mariposa Blues

Ron Koertge. Little, Brown, 1991. 171p. Hardbound (ISBN 0-316-50103-4) $15.95. **Grades 7–12. 3Q, 2P.**
Reviewed in: HB, 7/8/91, p. 464; PW, 5/10/91, p. 284; SLJ, 5/91, p. 111.

Graham was definitely feeling weird. It seemed like he was always in a crappy mood and arguing with his dad over everything. He had been looking forward to spending the summer at Mariposa Downs, the race track in southern California, surfing and helping his dad with the horses he trained. But whatever had been bothering him had come along with him. And things weren't so perfect with Leslie anymore, even though she had been his best friend for years. Her dad was a horse trainer too, and Graham and Leslie had hung out together every summer. But now Leslie was all excited about this guy she'd met in San Francisco. "Todd is so cool . . . ," "He looks like a Greek god . . . ," "He's talented, sensitive, and vulner-

able"—and he's coming to Mariposa Downs. Graham could hardly wait!

With all that going on, Graham had been sure the summer couldn't get worse. He was wrong. He and his dad got into a really big argument over a horse named Pepperoni. If Graham was wrong and Pepperoni ended up dead, his dad would never forgive him, but what was worse was that Graham would never forgive himself.

—*Marianne Tait Pridemore*
San Jose Public Library, San Jose, CA

Me and the End of the World

William Corbin. Simon & Schuster, 1991. 222p. Hardbound (ISBN 0-671-74223-X) $15.00. **Grades 5–8. 3Q, 3P.**

What would you do if you knew the world was going to end in four months? [Ask your audience for some answers if you wish and then proceed.]

Tim is in just this predicament—the world is going to end in four months. Everyone's saying it, and it's even all over the newspapers. Tim's considered what he wants to do about this, and has decided that before the end of the world, he has to accomplish four things he's wanted to do for a long time, but just kept putting off.

First, he has to fight Dunk Bolander, the enormous bully who's been picking on him for weeks now.

Second, he wants to hitch sled rides with his best friend, Ed, on this exciting new route they have planned.

Third, he has to apologize to Mr. Weinstock for being a coward about a racial slur that was scrawled on his sidewalk.

And finally, he wants to kiss Judy Felton.

How would you go about deciding what you *really* wanted to do before your world ended? More importantly, how would you go about *doing* them? That's the point Tim's at now. He doesn't quite know how he's going to accomplish these four things. All of them take courage, maybe more courage than Tim thinks he has.

What about you—would you have the courage to do the four most important things in your life before the end of the world?

—*C. Allen Nichols*
Rocky River Public Library, Rocky River, OH

Mean Streak

Ilene Cooper. Morrow, 1991. 190p. Hardbound (ISBN 0-688-0843-1) $13.95. **Grades 5–8. 3Q, 3P.**

Veronica Volner has an image to keep up—the image that she's popular and happy, that it's okay that her parents are divorced, that she's really excited about her father's upcoming marriage. But the truth is that Veronica is angry and miserable. She lost her best friend over an argument about a boy, and she's not close to any of the girls she hangs around with. She doesn't want her father to get married again. She doesn't like his girlfriend and has no intention of ever getting along with her.

Veronica thinks her image is perfect, that no one can see how she really feels. So when someone sees through her lies and dares to feel sorry for her, Veronica arranges a nasty little scheme. But when her scheme backfires, Veronica comes face to face with her own ugly mean streak, and can't hide behind her image any longer.

—*Janice Lauer*
Allan Frear Elementary, Camden, DE

📖 The Moon of the Gray Wolves

Jean Craighead George. Nonfiction. Harper-Collins, 1991 (rev. ed.). 48p. Hardbound (ISBN 0-06-022442-8) $14.95. **Grades 3–6. 4Q, 3P.**

November is the moon of the gray wolf. In the harsh wilderness of Alaska, it is also a month that the wolves must struggle to survive, for it is the month when the bitter cold of the long, dark winter closes in.

The black wolf is the leader of the four adult wolves and the five pups that make up his pack. The life of a wolf is hard and dangerous. Only the strong and cunning can survive, and not all of the pups will see the end of this November moon.

The black wolf raises his voice in song. One by one, the members of his pack join in. He sings the hunter's song, because the month of November is also the month of the great caribou migration. Other animals prick up their ears. To some, like the snowshoe hare, it's a signal to burrow deeper into their nests. To others—the fox, the owl, the raven, the magpie—the hunt song means food for all if the wolves are successful.

Go along with the wolf pack on its caribou hunt in the frozen November night. You may discover that the wolf is not really who its reputation says it is.

—*Diane Deuel*
Central Rappahannock Regional Library, Fredricksburg, VA

📖 Nekomah Creek

Linda Crew. Illustrated by Charles Robinson. Delacorte, 1991. 191p. Hardbound (ISBN 0-385-30442-0) $14.00. **Grades 3–6. 3Q, 3P.**

Robby Hummer lives on Nekomah Creek in Oregon and he thinks his family is normal. But the other kids at school aren't so sure. Is it normal for a dad to stay home and take care of the kids while the mom goes to work? Is

it normal for a dad to like to cook? Is it normal for a nine-year-old boy to have to see the school counselor because he likes to read more than he likes to play sports?

Robby is afraid that the school counselor will think his family is weird, just like all the kids at school do. He's afraid that she's going to make him leave his family and live in a foster home. How can he make his weird family look normal enough to please her?

—*Melanie Witulski*
Toledo-Lucas County Public Library, Toledo, OH

📖 Next Thing to Strangers

Sheri Cooper Sinykin. Lothrop, 1991. 147p. Hardbound (ISBN 0-688-10694-3) $12.95. **Grades 5–8. 3Q, 3P.**

Take one Arizona trailer park for retired people, two bored teenagers on winter break from school, and mix with two sets of peculiar grandparents. Stir in a few secrets, several problems, and some feelings of resentment, and you have the recipe for *Next Thing to Strangers*.

Cass McFerren's grandparents had sent for her. She hadn't seen or heard from them in eleven years, and the last time she saw them was at her father's funeral when she was three. The sunshine sounded good, the change of scenery sounded better, and warm, loving grandparents sounded best of all. Cass willingly left her mother in Iowa and headed for Arizona, ready for a terrific holiday.

But when she got there, Cass discovered that things were not at all what she had been expecting. Her grandparents were not the loving pair she'd hoped for. Grandfather seemed as hard as granite and Grandmother was fat and sickly. Their lack of warmth was exceeded only by the lack of any kind of food a teenager would want to eat. Did they really want her or not? Would she ever feel comfortable around them? How could she spend her entire vacation with these unloving, ancient people?

Muffin, Grandmother's little dog, was Cass's only chance for a little freedom. She needed to be taken for walks, and it was Cass's job to take her. It was on one of those walks that she met Jordy Sondel, another teenager visiting his grandparents, and both their vacations got a lot more interesting! But if Cass was going to make this vacation a success, she'd have to ignore some obvious problems: she caught Jordy injecting himself with something, the trailer park threatened to throw her out, and Grandmother wasn't just sickly—there was something really wrong with her. But whether this vacation could be called a success or not, one thing was certain—it was sure to be one holiday she would never forget!

—*Sue Young*
Ysleta Independent School District, El Paso, TX

📖 Night of Reunion

Michael Allegretto. Avon, 1991. 276p. Paperbound (ISBN 0-380-71442-6) $4.99. Scribner's, 1990. 256p. Hardbound (ISBN 0-684-19133-4) $17.95. **Grades 9–12, adults. 4Q, 4P.**

Sarah knew something was wrong as soon as she saw the look on Alex's face when he read the letter. She had never seen Alex react to anything the way he reacted to this letter. After he left the room, taking the letter with him, Sarah picked up the envelope. The return address—Joseph Pomeroy—told her little until she remembered that Pomeroy had been Alex's first wife's maiden name. Sarah knew very little about the marriage; Alex had understandably gotten quiet and depressed when he'd briefly told her about the terrible automobile accident that had killed his wife and son. It made no sense that a letter from his former father-in-law could be so upsetting. Sarah decided not to ask Alex about what the letter said. She would just wait until he was ready to share it with her. The next evening he began by saying, "Sarah, I'm afraid that I haven't been completely honest with you." That alone was enough to frighten her, but what Alex revealed next was far, far worse than she could ever have imagined.

His first wife had not been killed in an auto accident. She had been murdered, along with their two-year-old adopted son. They had been brutally slaughtered by Christine Helstrum, a woman the courts declared an insane psychopath, the natural mother of the little boy she killed. She had physically abused him so severely that the courts had taken him away from her and put him up for adoption. Enraged that her son had been taken away from her, Christine tracked him down and killed him and his adoptive mother. She had been sent to a state mental institution, presumably for the rest of her life. Alex was at the sentencing, and after the sentence had been given, she screamed at him that she would escape and come after him and kill him for taking her son away from her. Alex, and others, had had no doubt that she meant what she said. And now it seemed like she was going to make good on her threat, because she'd escaped from the mental hospital, and was considered to be very dangerous.

Sarah listened to Alex in horror. Would they become Christine's next victims? Even though they don't live in the same town, it was still possible that she could find them. Suddenly, their home was full of strange noises and disturbing events, all subtly threatening. Had Christine found them already? Was she waiting, watching, planning to destroy Alex's family all over again? Was she planning a night of reunion—a night of death?

—Helen Schlichting
Sac Community School, Sac City, IA

📖 The Night the Whole Class Slept Over

Stella Pevsner. Clarion, 1991. 162p. Hardbound (ISBN 0-899-19983-6) $13.95. **Grades 5–8. 3Q, 3P.**

Everyone in the sixth grade is looking forward to the annual Christmas vacation sleepover at the Lake Lorraine Public Library. They'll spend the whole night reading, telling stories, eating, and eventually, sleeping.

One particular sixth-grader, Dan Wakefield, is really excited about the sleepover. He's lived lots of places before moving to Lake Lorraine, because his artist parents are always searching for the perfect place to live. Now he's hoping that his parents will abandon their plans to move to a log cabin near the U.S.-Canadian border and settle permanently in Lake Lorraine, near his grandparents. He's had enough of moving around and has made some friends he doesn't want to leave: Felix, who is a whiz at computers; BJ, who wants to be an entertainer; and Amanda, who surprises Dan with her beautiful smile. Dan is sure the sleepover will be the highlight of his year, especially if his parents do decide to move north.

When the day of the sleepover dawns, it is gray and dismal and snowy. The snowflakes are the kind that sting when the wind blows them into your face, but the gloomy weather can't dampen Dan's high spirits. His parents are going to look at a house for sale and his grandparents are going to play bridge at their club, so Dan has to baby-sit for his two-year-old sister Martha. But this doesn't diminish his excitement either. Even when his grandparents are delayed by the snow and he has to take Martha to the library with him, Dan is still bubbling with enthusiasm.

However, none of the sixth-graders anticipating a night of fun and games has any idea what kinds of things will happen during *The Night the Whole Class Slept Over*.

—Terrie Ratcliffe
Irving Public Library, Irving, TX

📖 Not the End of the World

Rebecca Stowe. Pantheon, 1991. 151p. Hardbound (ISBN 0-679-40945-9) $18.00. **Grades 7–12. 3Q, 3P.**

I hate being a girl, even if it is pretty important if I'm ever going to be the first woman governor of Michigan. But I really *hate* being a girl. When I was a little kid, I'd say my prayers and ask God to bless everyone I knew, not just the people I loved ('cause they weren't always the same thing), and then I'd ask Him to please make me a boy. Maybe if I'd been a boy, I wouldn't have gotten into all that trouble in school last year. And that trouble is the reason I have to go to summer school with all the delinquents and dumbheads when I'm not really either of those things. I'm just different. Grandmother says I do things just to be different, but what she doesn't know—what nobody knows—is that the reason I'm different is that I'm not just me. There are six different people inside me, and one of them is even a boy! It's not that I'm crazy or anything, it's just that these other people are like a part of me that I keep locked up inside me all the time, only sometimes I go away and they come out and take over. And last year when all that trouble was going on, the others were there and helped me. Of course, they didn't stop me from taking all the medicines in the bathroom cabinet. I did that. I took it all, Ex-Lax and everything. Only I didn't die, I just got sick and had to stay home all day with Grandmother. That wasn't death, that was Purgatory! And no one even knew I did it—I guess they just thought my mother didn't shop that well.

Grandmother says I'm possessed by the devil, and if he isn't out by the time I'm 13 my soul will be lost. I don't know . . . I'm not sure I've got much soul left after what happened last year anyway . . . .

—*Marijo Duncan*
Phoenix Public Library, Phoenix, AZ

Nothing But the Truth

Avi. Orchard, 1991. 177p. Hardbound
(ISBN 0-531-08559-7) $14.99. **Grades 5–12**
(J. Bray); 7–12 (P. Jones). 4Q, 3P.

The headline in the *Manchester Record* read: "SUS-PENDED FOR PATRIOTISM" and the byline was "by J. Stewart, Education Reporter."

"While it may appear to be an April Fool's Day joke, tenth-grader Philip Malloy of Harrison High School was suspended for singing 'The Star-Spangled Banner.'

"His parents, Susan and Benjamin Malloy of Harrison Township, do not consider themselves super-patriots, but they did raise their son to have pride in his country. It was only natural, then, for Philip to sing along when the national anthem was played on tape during morning exercises. According to Harrison School's superintendent, Dr. A. Seymour, there is no rule against singing the anthem. Indeed, in every other class Philip did just that. His new homeroom teacher, Ms. Margaret Narwin, however, changed the rules. Every time Philip lifted his voice to sing she threw him out of class, insisting he was creating a disturbance during the national anthem.

"School principal Dr. Gertrude Doane, who admits that Philip has no previous bad marks on his record, saw the issue only as one of discipline, and referred all questions regarding school policy to Dr. Joseph Palleni, the assistant principal. Dr. Palleni, however, refused to be interviewed regarding the incident.

"What will young Malloy—who has his own delivery route for the *Manchester Record*—do during his suspension from school? Philip, who still hopes to make the school track team this spring, said 'Try to keep up with my work, and work out with classmates after school.'

"Harrison Township will be voting on a new school district budget this spring, along with a new school board."

Do you believe everything you read in the newspapers? Well, maybe not the article in the tabloids called "I was Bigfoot's Bride's Second Husband's Cousin from Venus." But what about what you read in your local paper? The reporter's job is to report the facts, all the facts, and nothing but the facts, right? So what are the facts in this article?

1. Fact: Philip Malloy was suspended for singing the national anthem. Not true.

2. Fact: There is no rule against singing the national anthem. Wrong.

3. Fact: Philip could and did sing the anthem in every other class. Not true.

4. Fact: Philip's homeroom teacher, Ms. Narwin, threw him out every time he tried to sing. False.

5. Fact: Philip sang the national anthem. Not entirely true.

What are the facts? What is the truth? Read this book, and find out the truth, the whole truth, and nothing but the truth!

—*Julie Bray*
Jasper County Public Library, Rensselaer, IN

The Court of Public Opinion is now in session. First witness, please state your name, your occupation, and your version of the events that took place at Harrison High.

"My name is Philip Malloy. I'm a ninth-grader at Harrison and I got suspended for singing the national anthem. I'm kinda patriotic and so I like to sing along when they play the recording of 'The Star-Spangled Banner' every morning. I mean it doesn't hurt anything. But this teacher, Mrs. Narwin, yelled at me to stop. She's got something against me. I don't know what it is. They got this dumb rule about being quiet. I mean, what about free speech—what about my rights?"

Next witness, please.

"My name is Margaret Narwin and I've been teaching at Harrison High School for 21 years. I love literature and love to teach it, even if today's student doesn't really care. It's almost as if I am out of touch with contemporary teaching and students like Philip Malloy. A bright young man who has some sort of personal problem. It causes him to act up in class with his loud disrespectful singing of the national anthem, which disrupts the whole class. It's disrespectful! But I never wanted him suspended! That was the assistant principal's choice, not mine. I guess as a teacher I don't have any rights at all, do I?"

Next witness, please.

"My name is Joseph Palleni. I'm the assistant principal at Harrison High in charge of student discipline. You wouldn't believe the problems we have—drugs, violence, all sorts of things. Why? Because kids won't follow the rules. So when Philip came into my office I told him, look, we try to be flexible, but rules are rules. If a student creates a disturbance in class, that is breaking a rule. An important rule. So I told Philip to apologize, and he wouldn't. So I suspended him, not because he sang the national anthem, but because he broke a rule and wouldn't apologize. When a kid creates a disturbance, then other students can't learn, and I have to watch out for those students' right to learn."

Next witness, please.

"My name is Jennifer Stewart and I'm the education reporter for the *Manchester Record*. Got a call from a friend of Philip's family to tell me about his being suspended. So I started making phone calls—superintendent, principal, assistant principal, teacher, and Philip. I got everyone's side of the story. I printed the article in the paper, then the wire services picked it up, and then the national media and the talk shows. That's what this country is all about—newspapers printing the truth under the First Amendment protection of freedom of the press."

You, the Court of Public Opinion, have heard the witnesses and now you must decide. Please rise, put your hands over your hearts, and repeat after me: "Do you swear to tell the truth, the whole truth, and nothing but the truth?" But tell me, who's right here and who's wrong? And tell me, if everyone tells one side of the story, and the stories don't all match, then is someone lying, or can all of them be telling nothing but the truth?

—Patrick Jones
Allen County Public Library, Fort Wayne, IN

Quiver River

David Carkeet. HarperCollins, 1991. 236p.
Hardbound (ISBN 0-060-22453-3) $14.95.
Grades 7–12. 4Q, 3P.

The boredom must have gotten to Ricky. He certainly never planned to join in the traditional Miwok Indian deer chase. After all, he was at camp to work a summer job, not cavort around the lake like his older brother!

Gradually Ricky increased the distance between himself and the closest college student on the chase. When Maggie disappeared, Ricky began to feel like he was alone on the mountain. The climb got so steep that he was forced to pull himself up with his hands. Then he cleared the top of a ridge. The view was breathtaking. Ricky paused on a flat rock to rest and soak in the beauty.

The silence was shattered when a deer broke through the brush. Ricky and his quarry stood face to face, staring into each other's eyes. Then the deer bounded off again and Ricky took off after him. Thinking on his feet, Ricky ran down the mountain on an angled path. There was a slim chance he could cut the deer off lower on the slope. Running down a rock-strewn mountain wasn't easy. Ricky expected to fall over a rock or bush at every step, but the bushes seemed to create a path before him. Strangely, though, the path funneled into a maze. It took a turn uphill, and Ricky sprinted for a hump of earth. He cleared it with a flying leap—and that leap took him into the yawning gorge of Quiver River.

[You can stop here for a shorter talk—**Ed.**]

Some people have said that their lives flashed before their eyes when they faced death. Ricky's didn't. He wasn't scared, he was just plain angry. His brother had gotten him into this mess.

But the brush-walled path hadn't lead to a cliff by accident, and Ricky's brother hadn't made it. It and the maze were just two more peculiar signs of the Miwok's presence in the mountains.

What had happened to Ricky's quiet summer cleaning the campgrounds at Quiver Lake? Was the culprit a modern Miwok, a college student, a madman, or a spirit trapped in time?

—Bernice D. Crouse
Fulton County Library, McConnellsburg, PA

Red Sky in the Morning

Andrea Wyman. Holiday House, 1991. 225p.
Hardbound (ISBN 0-823-40903-1) $13.95.
Grades 5–8. 3Q, 2P.

Red sky in the morning, sailors take warning. What a way to start a day, or a lifetime.

Calista Common is an unusual name, even for a 14-year-old living in Indiana in 1909. But Calista doesn't mind—she's an unusual girl who's had to face some unusual challenges during her 14 years. Calista's mother dies during childbirth, she loses her sister's friendship because she has to go to work, she comes to love her grandfather more than anyone else in the world, and she discovers that her father is not the man her whole family believed him to be.

Red sky at night, shepherds' delight. What a way to end a day or end a part of your life, not knowing what the dawn will bring to the sky or to your life. Find out what happened to Calista on the way to Oregon, when she has her red sky at night, and what changes the dawn will bring to her and her family.

—Barbara Flottmeier
LaCrosse Public Library, LaCrosse, WI

The Remarkable Journey of Prince Jen

Lloyd Alexander. Dutton, 1991. 273p. Hardbound (ISBN 0-525-44826-8) $14.95. **Grades 5–8. 3Q, 2P.**

"It is a remarkable kingdom. Far north of here, in its great capital, Ch'ung-chao, reigns the noblest and most generous of rulers: Yuan-ming. His subjects thrive and prosper, the land yields harvests in abundance, the arts flourish as richly as the orchards. The laws are just, but seldom enforced, since the inhabitants deal with each other as they themselves would wish to be dealt with. Thus, few officials are needed, but they serve their monarch and the people well."

Young Prince Jen sets off on a most remarkable journey to the kingdom of T'ien-kuo and the city of Ch'ung-chao. And old Master has chosen six gifts for Jen to offer Yuan-ming when he arrives in Ch'ung-chao: a saddle, a sword, a paint box, a bowl, a kite, and a flute. Worried that these items are unworthy of such a wise and worthy ruler, Prince Jen is surprised to discover that amazing truths exist in even the simplest of gifts. But his journey also teaches him lessons, because from the moment he rescues an old man from the river, he must deal with an ever-increasing number of obstacles.

Jen loses two of his gifts and his army escort. The sword is stolen at the beginning of his journey, and he must fight Natha Yellow Scarf to get it back. A storm sweeps him away in the river and robs him of his true identity. But all his adventures serve to teach him the one real truth, the truth that is able to make a young prince into a wiser and stronger person, and perhaps someday, a wise and strong ruler, just like the one who now rules T'ien-kuo so nobly and so well.

—*Cara A. Waits*
Tempe Public Library, Tempe, AZ

Safari Adventure

Dick Houston. Nonfiction. Cobblehill Books, 1991. 145p. Hardbound (ISBN 0-525-65051-2) $15.95. **Grades 7–12, adults. 4Q, 2P.** Reviewed in: SLJ, 11/91, p. 139; Science Bks & Films, 11/91, p. 234.

It's never to late to make your childhood dreams come true. Dick Houston, African safari leader, knows that better than many of us.

Growing up in Ohio in the 1950s, Dick was fascinated by the documentary films on Africa made by Martin and Osa Johnson during the 1920s and 30s. The Johnsons weren't tourists, they were adventurers, free to go when and where they wanted, filming animals and really getting to know the country. Dick decided then that the life of an adventurer was the one for him, and was determined to one day have his own adventure safari. Even when he became a teacher, he never really gave up his dream, although he didn't start working to make it into reality until one of his students challenged him to do just that.

Dick went to Africa and began to make his dream come true with a few short camping trips in the bush, but he still wanted to lead a true safari like the Johnsons'. When he met Jack Thornton, a young Britisher who'd driven overland from England to East Africa, Dick knew he'd found the partner he needed to recreate the safaris he'd admired so much as a child. Dick's safari became a reality with a month-long trip into the East African bush—an adventure as well as a dream come true for six clients who were also part of the working team.

One day, while taking pictures of Kilimanjaro during a spectacular sunrise, the group became so absorbed in what they were doing that they didn't see the small band of elephants 400 feet away. The elephants didn't seem interested in the people, so the members continued their filming.

Suddenly Dick realized that one of the elephants had veered towards them and was about 200 feet away. The film group had strayed about 200 yards away from the relative safety of the camp. He told the group not to make any sudden moves and to slowly work their way back to camp. Certainly the elephant would stop . . . . It did, about 170 feet away, looking down over upthrust tusks and unfurling its gigantic ears. When it resumed its slow advance, Dick looked frantically for trees to climb or at least hide behind. Suddenly, the elephant gave an ear-shattering trumpet, lowered its head, flattened its ears against its sides, and charged the group.

Dick shouted, "Now's the time to run!" Sprinting like Kentucky Derby entrants, they ran for camp, with the elephant rapidly closing the distance between them—75 feet, 50 feet, 30 feet! The adventurers dove through the open doors of the Land Rover and waited for the impact of the pachyderm . . . .

Sign on for a safari with Dick Houston, and discover one of the last wild frontiers on earth!

—*Kristina Peters*
Carroll County Public Library, Greenmount, MD

Imagine you're driving your truck along a dusty desert road in Kenya, East Africa. The land is covered with low, thick bushes that aren't much protection from the sun, and the temperature's at least 112 degrees. In the distance you can see the green rolling hills that lead up to a beautiful high mountaintop. That's your goal—reaching the lovely cool shade of the mountain slope before your limited supply of water runs out.

Suddenly, a purple-legged ostrich bursts out of the bushes to run alongside your truck. You go faster. So does he. He gets in front of your truck, running high and proud before you, like a feathered drum major. You and your friends burst out laughing—you're back in the band!

Another day, tired of the heat, you decide to climb Mount Kilimanjaro. Halfway up, at about 8,000 feet, you discover that you and your friends aren't the only ones trying to get away from the heat—there are elephants trotting through the trees. It's not only cooler, there's lots of vegetation for them to eat.

But you have to spend time in town, too, stocking up on supplies. Walking the streets of Nairobi, you remember that they are the same streets that Ernest Hemingway once walked, preparing for another expedition into the bush, just as you are.

This time, you're off to a game reserve to watch thousands of wildebeests on the move, leaping gazelles and zebras, or lions stalking their prey. Remember to put all your food away after dinner. There are plenty of elephants and baboons that know where your camp is—and they're hungry!

Finally, you head for Kenya's coastline, to wash off the dust with a swim in the ocean. Then there's a picnic on the beach, with spicy rice and fish, shish kabob, fruit, and coconut milk. Lying on the sand, the snowy peaks and the dusty desert seem very far away.

You can do all this, and more, when you join Dick Houston, who's made his dreams of adventure come true, leading safaris in Africa. And even though he admits that adventure can sometimes be uncomfortable, not to mention dangerous, he and his fellow adventurers wouldn't trade it for anything!

—Mark Anderson
Fairfax County Public Library, Fairfax, VA

Sammy Carducci's Guide to Women

Ronald Kidd. Dutton, 1991. 99p. Hardcover (ISBN 0-525-67363-6) $14.95. **Grades 5–8. 4Q, 4P.**

At last there's a complete guide to women—according to Sammy Carducci, that is. That is, if you want to accept advice about women from a four-foot, two-inch sixth-grader who wears a suit, tie, and high-top sneakers to school every day. But that's Sammy for you. He owes everything he knows about women to his older brother Nick. Nick is 19 and sells insurance, and Sammy has spent hours watching him with women and listening to him talk about how to deal with women.

But not even Sammy's best friend Gus will take Sammy seriously. Gus likes to make forts out of his mashed potatoes—or whatever other food he happens to be eating—more than he likes girls. Instead of taking notes

about important information Sammy is giving him about women, Gus draws a rocket ship with his four-color pen.

Sammy decides to give up on Gus and give himself the benefit of all his knowledge. After surveying all the women in school, Sammy decides on Becky Davidson, five foot six, and begins his attempt to win her heart. But he has a real rival in Kevin Reynolds, who's five foot eight, fourteen years old, goes to Brentwood Prep, wears a letter jacket, and wants Becky for himself.

Will Sammy's theories about women work on Becky Davidson? Find out in *Sammy Carducci's Guide to Women.*

—Marilyn Eanes
Round Rock Independent School District, Austin, TX

Seven Long Years Until College

Mary Jane Auch. Holiday House, 1991. 169p. Hardbound (ISBN 0-8234-0901-5) $13.95. **Grades 5–6. 4Q, 4P.**

My sister, Christa, is really lucky. She gets to go to college at Corinthia and live in a dorm. She doesn't have to stay at home and live with Frank. Frank is Mom's new husband. Boy, talk about opposites attracting! Mom's a laid-back, fun-loving person who has absolutely no organizational skills. Frank is a perfectionist with absolutely no imagination and no sense of humor. Boring is the word that best describes him. He's a real stuffed shirt. Add his bossy, snobbish mother to the picture, and you've got a better idea of what I have to put up with. Nothing Mom or I do suits Mrs. Willderby. Mom's acting like a real wimp around the old lady, but not me. I'm not going to let her push me around, and I'm not going to make myself over just to suit her either! Oh, how I wish I were going away to college like Christa. I really miss her, and my best friend Carla is moving away soon, so I won't have her to talk to either. I think it's going to be a long seven years till college. I just hope I can last that long!

—Kathy Ann Miller
SLIM student, Emporia State University, Emporia, KS

Skymaze

Gillian Rubinstein. Orchard, 1991. 183p. Hardbound (ISBN 0-531-05929-4) $14.95. **Grades 5–8. 4Q, 4P.**

Have you ever felt the urge to leap into a computer game and actually become one of the characters? That's exactly what happens to Ben, Elaine, Andrew, and Mario as they insert the Skymaze disk and grasp the joystick. It seemed to be an exciting maze involving physical and mental skill, with hard but steady progression from one level to the next. The irresistible challenge is to solve the maze using the unique gifts of unlimited time, flying, and healing that the game bestows on its players. The only problems are finding times and places to play, and keeping the game a secret from Andrew's stepbrother.

But then two new players suddenly enter the game and make bad choices, activating the Pale Guardians and the Dark Clouds. This gives power to evil and fearful things and the game becomes a desperate race to save a life.

If you read *Space Demons*, you'll love this sequel to it. What do you think—still want to jump into a computer game?

—*Bette Ammon*
Missoula Public Library, Missoula, MT

Soccer Shock

Donna Jo Napoli. Illustrated by Meredith Johnson. Dutton, 1991. 184p. Hardbound (ISBN 0-525-44827-6) $13.95. **Grades 3–6. 3Q, 3P.**

Oh my gosh! What's that I hear? It's my two favorite freckles talking to each other. Ever since I almost got hit by that bolt of lightning, strange things have been happening to me.

It all started when I was hurrying home from soccer practice, and I got knocked down by a bolt of lightning. When I woke up, I could hear voices, but it wasn't until later that I realized that it was Gilbert and Frankie talking to each other about me. When I told the doctor I was hearing voices, he said that I'd be okay and told my mom to keep an eye on me for a few days.

And now that's the problem—everybody is watching me. My mother says I'm acting strange. My sister thinks I'm crazy because I told her I can now hear my freckles talk, since my ears are extra-sensitive from the lightning bolt. Kim, a girl at school, looks at me as though she's awe-struck, and my new best friend, Grayson, thinks I'm proving to the kids at school that I'm a brainy nerd because I cut holes in my sweats, tape myself with tape from freckle to freckle, and talk to myself all the time.

What he doesn't understand is that I'm *not* talking to myself. I'm talking to Gilbert, my favorite freckle that's on my knee. He's the freckle that communicates with all of the other freckles on my body. And he's also the freckle that's going to help me make the soccer team.

Well, I guess Grayson is going to help a lot, too. He's so good at soccer, and he's offered to help me learn if I'll help him with math. It's a good deal because he's really not dumb, like some of the kids say. It's just that, at first, he doesn't understand, but he does after I relate math to playing soccer.

Then there's Kim. She keeps doing things to get me in trouble—at least it looks that way. Grayson says she likes me and is just trying to get my attention.

I don't know about that, but I do know that talking to my freckles, keeping my mother off my back, making my sister promise not to tell about my freckles, and keeping Grayson from getting mad at me when Kim paints daisies on his favorite soccer ball—the one he loaned me—all keep my life in a state of total chaos.

But here I go blabbering on, and you really don't know what's going on. But you'll find out when you read my book, and you might even wish you could talk to your freckles too.

—*Donna Houser*
School District 257, Iola, KS

Soup in Love

Robert Newton Peck. Illustrated by Charles Robinson. Delacorte, 1991. 114p. Hardbound (ISBN 0-385-30563-X) $14.00. **Grades 5–8. 3Q, 4P.**

Soup's back and he's in love. Soup and Peck are at it again, and this time they've discovered a new game even better than baseball—Smooch.

Everyone in the village of Learning is getting ready for Valentine's Day by decorating the whole village with red paper hearts. There's going to be a prize for the best valentine and naturally, Soup wants to win. He has plans that Peck is not sure he even wants to hear about. But the valentine they construct surprises the entire village, including Soup and Peck! Just imagine what they could do with a refrigerator crate, an old sign, some old Christmas decorations, and a horse!

Find out about the game of Smooch and one of the most surprising valentines ever created in *Soup in Love*.

—*Marilyn Eanes*
Round Rock Independent School District, Austin, TX

Spirit House

William Sleator. Dutton, 1991. 134p. Hardbound (ISBN 0-525-44814-4) $13.95. **Grades 7–12. 3Q, 4P.**

Julie was not looking forward to having a Thai exchange student stay as a house guest. No sir, this was not going to be fun. He was probably as geeky as they come. Julie was even more convinced after she saw his letter, with his ever-so-correct English and the polite way he talked about Julie and her family. Yish, a *total* geek. And his picture— even geekier!

It was no wonder she didn't recognize him when he got off the plane. He not only wasn't a geek, he was just plain gorgeous—and fun! Julie refused to think about why he was so different from the person they'd been expecting. So his English was a little broken, not at all like the letter he'd written, but hey, he was learning. There's a lot of difference between being able to write in a foreign language and being able to speak it.

It wasn't until Julie's little brother built a spirit house in the back yard that things really began to get strange. The spirit house was supposed to make Bia feel more at home, because, now that they had a place to live, the spirits could follow him from Thailand to America. But almost from the very moment he saw the spirit house, Bia changed. He'd been so friendly to Julie, and even given her a special Buddha pendant he always wore. Suddenly Bia acted like he didn't even know Julie was alive, let alone special. He was different with everyone else, too, acting almost as if he were afraid. But who, or what, could he be afraid of?

It was almost like Bia was three different people—the geek who wrote the letter; the handsome, charming young man who got off the plane; and the scared and nervous guy who was with them now. Which one was the *real* Bia, and what did the spirit house have to do with his changing?

—*Marijo Duncan*
Phoenix Public Library, Phoenix, AZ

A Summer on Thirteenth Street

Charlotte Herman. Dutton, 1991. 181p. Hard-bound (ISBN 0-525-44642-7) $13.95. **Grades 5–6. 4Q, 3P.**

It is the summer of 1944, and everywhere you look in Chicago you can see signs of the war. Sailors from the nearby naval base stroll along streets lined with fluttering American flags.

Shirley Cohen is 11 years old, and summer is her favorite time of year. She's looking forward to chocolate malteds, softball, picnics in the park, and playing with her best friend, Morton. But this summer is different, because the war reaches Shirley, her family, her friends, and her neighborhood in many ways. Some of the changes are small, like the flags with blue or gold stars in the windows of families whose sons or daughters have gone to war. Other changes are bigger, like the air-raid practices they all have to participate in.

Shirley and her friends decide to help the war effort by planting a victory garden in one corner of her yard. The summer still seems ideal, until the reality of the war begins to intrude. Manny, their favorite soda jerk, enlists and is dead before the summer is over. They're sure the local handyman with the funny accent is a German spy, and their attempts to expose him lead to an embarrassing confrontation.

Yes, summer is Shirley's favorite time of year, but the summer of 1944 is different. It means death and war and having to grow up too soon and too fast.

—*Cynthia L. Lopuszynski*
Lafayette, IN

Tails of the Bronx

Jill Pinkwater. Macmillan, 1991. 208p. Hard-bound (ISBN 0-027-74652-6) $14.95. **Grades 5–6. 3Q, 4P.**

There's no place on earth like the Bronx. It's part of New York City, and I live there. My name is Loretta Bernstein. I live on Burnridge Avenue. Burnridge Avenue is a special neighborhood. We all watch out for one another here—especially the bunch I hang out with.

So when the cats in the neighborhood began to disappear, everyone noticed. But what's more important is that the kids I hang out with, all seven of us, decided to get to the bottom of the missing cats mystery. We were determined to do it even if it meant starting with an investigation of the neighborhood witch's house!

We became sleuths. We pooled our resources. We pursued each clue, and in the process we made some surprising discoveries about our neighborhood. Why don't you come along and help us track down the *Tails of the Bronx*?

—*Olivia Jacobs*
Wichita High School North, Wichita, KS

Tatham Mound

Piers Anthony. Morrow, 1991. 522p. Hard-bound (ISBN 0-688-10140-2) $22.00. **Grades 9–12, adults. 3Q, 1P.**

Hotfoot's first raid against an enemy tribe changed his life forever. On it, he killed his first man—with an arrow shot point-blank into his enemy's throat—and came to be known as Throat Shot. On it, he was permanently maimed by his enemy's arrow as he narrowly escaped capture. On it, the spirits of the dead gifted him with the ability to learn new languages quickly, and to talk with them. On it, the spirits also gave Throat Shot a mission to save his tribe from doom.

In the hope of fulfilling his mission, Throat Shot apprentices himself to an Indian trader and travels throughout his known world. He meets many other tribes and learns their languages. He visits their burial mounds and asks the spirits there to help him on his quest. He becomes a respected trader in his own right and proves himself to be fearless and loyal. He loves and marries two women, and he sees his family and friends killed by a mysterious illness.

Through it all, Throat Shot continues to converse with the spirits, attempting to fulfill the quest they have given him.

Talking is what Throat Shot does best, and to the many tribes he visits, he becomes known as Tale Teller, the historian, the legend maker, the news bringer. Finally, when Tale Teller becomes the interpreter for the Spanish Conquistador, de Soto, the doom that the spirits foretold comes true.

Is it possible to survive the promise of the spirits? Will Tale Teller be able to save his tribe and complete his mission, or will he be part of their destruction?

—Sue Padilla
Ida Long Goodman Memorial Library, St. John, KS

Time Windows

Kathryn Reiss. Harcourt Brace Jovanovich, 1991. 260p. Hardbound (ISBN 0-152-88205-7) $15.95. **Grades 5–8. 4Q, 3P.**

"I'm going to die!" screamed a voice in Miranda's head. Waves of terror washed over her and Miranda flung herself away from the dollhouse window. Standing shakily, she looked around frantically for the little girl she had seen through the window. The wads of paper Miranda had put down on the floor as a test lay just where the little girl had been, but she was nowhere to be seen.

It was true, then! Miranda couldn't understand it, but it was somehow true. When she looked through the dollhouse windows, her own attic vanished and an attic from another time appeared. Forcing back the terror that still churned in her stomach, Miranda walked back to the dollhouse and leaned down to look again through the tiny windows . . . .

What Miranda sees through the dollhouse windows both delights and terrifies her. In time, the terror she first felt will grow, as she realizes that events from the house's past are happening again. And to stop the evil, Miranda must relive it.

—Julie Bray
Jasper County Public Library, Rensselaer IN

To Venture Further

Tristan Jones. Nonfiction. Hearst Marine Books, 1991. 302p. Hardbound (ISBN 0-688-08022-7) $22.00. **Grades 9–12, adults. 3Q, 3P.**

Tristan Jones wanted to find the legendary continent of Atlantis. He even founded a society to do just that. Then, in 1982, one of his legs was amputated above the knee. Jones found himself living in the world of the physically disabled and decided it was too small for him. In an effort to make it larger, he decided to venture further, to try

something no one had ever attempted before. He set out to change the public's attitude toward the disabled by proving that not only could the disabled keep pace with the able-bodied, they could also do something that had never been done by *anyone.*

Because of his naval background, Jones decided to navigate a previously unconquered waterway. The challenge he chose was to cross the Isthmus of Kra, the thinnest part of the peninsula that includes Thailand. The crew he chose included his friend Thomas and three disabled Thai nationals. They were an unlikely group of five: two were small boys, three had missing limbs, one could not speak, one could hardly see beyond six feet, one was over 60 years old, and two were under 15. It seemed like the idea of a madman—five disabled people attempting to cross the Kra—a challenge that had defeated even the Japanese army. But Jones was on a quest to raise the disabled from the well of despair and prove that everyone needs to push their limits further and further out. To do that, he was ready to battle self and nature to earn a prize that nothing else could win.

—Helen Schlichting
Sac Community School, Sac City, IA

Two Moons in August

Martha Brooks. Joy Street Books, 1991. 199p. Hardbound (ISBN 0-316-10979-7) $14.95. **Grades 9–12, adults. 4Q, 4P.**

It's difficult at any age to deal with your mother's death, but at 15, how can you ever have a normal life without her? Your older sister moves back home, and she's certainly not normal! Your dad buries himself in his work, and hasn't the slightest idea what is going on in your life.

A year after her mother's death, Sidonie is still trying to deal with the loss and figure out just where her place in the world is. Her memories of her mother get mixed up with her everyday life as she tries to sort things out. Meeting Kieran, who's come to town for the summer, only adds to the confusion and frustration she feels.

Can Sidonie pick up the pieces of her shattered family life? Can anyone help her put them together again? Spend the summer with Sidonie and Kieran and find out.

—Judy McElwain
Laramie, WY

Unfinished Portrait of Jessica

Richard Peck. Delacorte, 1991. 162p. Hardbound (ISBN 0-385-30500-1) $15.00. **Grades 7–12, adults. 4Q, 3P.**

I'm so mad at my mother! She's run him off—I'll never forgive her. I had no idea when my father walked out that day that he was leaving her—and me! I keep wondering why he hasn't come back for me. He'll be back—I know it. He'll be back for me!

So when he does come back, I let him in, thinking that he'll ask me to pack my bags so I can leave with him. But he doesn't. He just grabs the portrait that his uncle, Lucius Pirie, the famous painter, gave our family. It's called the *Unfinished Portrait of Jessica*, and it's always hung over the mantel.

When he takes it, I figure I won't have to worry about what my mother will say when she sees that it's gone, since I'm sure I'll be going with my dad. But then he just leaves, and I'm left alone looking at the vacant space over the mantel. I decide I won't say a thing about the missing painting to my mother—I'll just wait till she asks me where it is. But the funny thing is, she never asks. Later, she tells me I'm going to visit my dad, who's now living in Mexico with his famous Uncle Lucius. I'm so excited I can hardly stand it! I'll have a chance to get away from my mother, live with my dad, and even meet his famous uncle.

But Mexico wasn't what I expected, and neither was my dad.

—*Donna Houser*
School District 257, Iola, KS

The Wild Rose

Doris Mortman. Bantam, 1991. 769p. Hardbound (ISBN 0-553-07419-9) $20.00. **Adults. 4Q, 3P.**

Katalin Gaspar stood nervously in the wings of the Opera Haz in Budapest, Hungary, awaiting her cue. Katalin went over her music in her head, her hands racing over an imaginary keyboard. She tried hard to calm herself. The performance had to be perfect tonight. To do less would arouse suspicion. The future of many people would depend on what happened here tonight.

Zoltan Gaspar took his place as the orchestra conductor. Tonight he would direct his daughter for the first time. The audience went wild when they saw him, and shouts of bravo filled the air. To them he was a survivor. He had endured the darkest times of Hungary's history, and he had won. The secret police had taken the music away from him when they crushed and crippled his hands. For many years there was no music, until he decided to take it back. Tonight was his triumphant return to the world of music.

This was to have been Laszlo Bohm's night to shine. He had planned this concert especially for Mikhail Gorbachev. He had been courting Gorbachev's support as the next leader of Hungary. Laszlo had been certain that he would be able to enlist that support, but Gorbachev had left Budapest suddenly, returning to Moscow without explanation. The tickets Laszlo had given him were being used by the secret police. When he saw them, Laszlo felt absolute terror course through him.

The gypsies had been camped out in the bowels of the Opera Haz for many days. Tonight they moved silently into place and waited for their cues. Tonight they would bring the ultimate degradation to a *gorgio*, a non-gypsy—they would claim her as one of their own.

Suddenly it was time. Katalin took her place at the piano. The music began. It was a perfect fusion of elements—composer, conductor, orchestra, and soloist. Together they attained a level of perfection that mesmerized the hall. As the third movement raced to its final crescendo, the music swelled in a triumphant roar. Its awesome power gripped the souls of everyone present, overwhelming the senses and obliterating all other sounds—including the click of a trigger.

—*Linda Olson*
Superior Public Library, Superior, WI

The Witch's Daughter

Nina Bawden. Houghton Mifflin, 1991. 184p. Hardbound (ISBN 0-395-58635-6) $13.95. **Grades 3–6. 3Q, 2P.**

"The witch's daughter sat on the rock in the bay. It was a huge rock, with steep sides of black basalt, turreted like a castle and crowned with purple heather. On one side the sea thundered, throwing up spray like white lace. Inland, the wet sand of low tide stretched back to the dunes and the brown slopes of Ben Luin beyond. The bay was empty except for a few bullocks at the water's edge and the gulls that swooped and cried like kittens over the shore and the hills of this Scottish island of Skua. The witch's daughter closed her eyes and flew with the gulls in the air: she turned and dived and felt the wind cold on her face . . . . Her name was Perdita, which means lost."

Painfully shy and lonely, Perdita has never been to school, never learned to read or write, and never had any friends or family. Except for Annie and Mr. Smith, the man who had hired Annie as a housekeeper, she associated with no one. Crossing paths with Tim and Janey was a chance to make friends, changing her future forever.

Tim and Janey could never have guessed what would be in store for them as they stepped off the steamer in Skuaphort. They often traveled with their botanist father on treks to find rare flowers, but this trip would prove to be more than a hunt for flowers. Crossing paths with Perdita would change their futures too, in ways no one could have suspected.

—*Cara A. Waits*
Tempe Public Library, Tempe, AZ

📖 Young Santa

Dan Greenburg. Illustrated by Warren Miller.
Viking, 1991. 72p. Hardbound (ISBN 0-670-83905-1) $13.95. **Grades 3–6. 3Q, 3P.**

Have you ever wondered about Santa Claus and how he got to be who he is today? After all, he wasn't born some fat old guy with a white beard, right? Right. So, what do you think Santa was like as a baby? A third-grader? Most important of all, what was he like as a teenager?

Look, here he is. [Show picture on page 21.] All dressed up in his red suit, delivering pizza in Hawaii. And here he is again. [Show picture on page 25.] He's in his red suit. He's in his sleigh. He's being pulled by eight tiny ra—walruses?! He's being pulled by eight tiny *walruses*? Whoever heard of that? Rudolph the Red-Nosed Walrus? How will a young and inexperienced Santa be able to figure this one out?

—Tracy Revel
Sussex Central Middle School, Millsboro, DE

Author Studies

A State-by-State Guide to Children's and Young Adult Authors and Illustrators
David V. Loertscher and Lance Castle

This concise, well-indexed guide to more than 4,000 authors and illustrators provides entries arranged by state of birth, alphabetically by author. Each entry contains name, birth and death dates, place of birth (actual birthplaces, not "adopted" states), and sample titles, as well as an index to additional information. An excellent "first resource" for information on authors and for help in finding information in reference tools.

**1991 344p. ISBN 0-931510-33-3
$37.50**
Also available on disk for MAC, Apple, and IBM. Call for details: 1-800-237-6124.

Biographical Index to Children's and Young Adult Authors and Illustrators
David V. Loertscher

This index to more than 13,000 authors, illustrators, poets, filmmakers, and cartoonists in both collective and single biographies is the most current available and the only one to include individiual biography and audiovisual resources as well. More than 1,500 biographical works are indexed. Entries include name, year of birth and death, country or state of birth, and sources.

**1992 v, 277p. ISBN 0-931510-40-6
$45.00**

An Author a Month (for Pennies)
Sharron L. McElmeel

Selected as "District's Choice 1988-1989" by **Curriculum Product News**.

A gem of a book.... Wonderful, wonderful!–**Teaching K-8**

Bring authors and children together in your library or classroom–for just pennies! Meet Marcia Brown, Tomie dePaola, Dr. Seuss, Arnold Lobel, Margot Zemach, Eric Carle, Bill Peet, Chris Van Allsburg, and others. Includes more than 700 activity suggestions designed to build reading by reading and reproducible photographs that are perfect for library display. K-6.

**1988 xviii, 224p.
ISBN 0-87287-661-6
$24.50**

An Author a Month (for Nickels)
Sharron L. McElmeel

Will fill the year with a wide variety of reading fun for students.– **Library Talk**

Introduce students to Pat Hutchins, John Steptoe, Hilary Knight, Tony Ross, and other beloved children's authors. Nine full author/illustrator units and three capsule units with hundreds of activity suggestions to fill the year with stimulating reading. K-6.

**1990 xiv, 172p. ISBN 0-87287-827-9
$24.00**

An Author a Month (for Dimes)
Sharron L. McElmeel

A wonderful new resource featuring Martha Alexander, Caroline Arnold, Graeme Base, Byrd Baylor, and other authors are brought to you and your students with photographs, biographical sketches, and inspiring activities for the library and classroom. K-6.

**1993 xiv, 185p.
ISBN 0-87287-952-6
$23.50**

Bookpeople: A First Album
Bookpeople: A Second Album
Sharron L. McElmeel

Useful tools for introducing children to "bookpeople" and for encouraging further reading.–**Booklist**

Welcome additions to the professional collection.–**School Library Media Activities Monthly**

Create a literature-rich environment and use the author/illustrator sections in the books as stimuli to further reading and writing. Poster pages (photographs and illustrations), background information on the authors, and suggestions for activities.

First Album
Includes Eve Bunting, Aliki, Jane Yolen, James Marshall, and others. Grades 1-4.
**1990 xiii, 176p.
ISBN 0-87287-720-5
$19.00**

Second Album
Covers Betsy Byars, Roald Dahl, Lynn Hall, Jean Fritz, and others. Grades 3-9.
**1990 xv, 200p. ISBN 0-87287-721-3
$20.00 ($24.00f)**

Bookpeople: A Multicultural Album
Sharron L. McElmeel

This exciting new multicultural album features 15 children's authors and illustrators who either belong to a minority culture or whose work authentically depicts a minority culture. Focusing on individuals such as Mitsumasa Anno, Virginia Driving Hawk Sneve, and Laurence Yep, it offers a unique approach to multiculturalism as well as a wealth of information to use in developing school reading programs.

**1992 xvii, 170p. ISBN 0-87287-953-4
$23.50**

Resources from Libraries Unlimited

Booktalking the Curriculum

By Lesley S. J. Farmer
San Domenico School, San Anselmo, CA

As teenagers enter high school, they have less time to read. Their homework load increases, they have many other recreational and sports activities, and for many, reading has become an uncool thing to do, especially if you actually enjoy it. They're more likely to peruse magazines than to find time for a long novel. In addition, many teachers use a textbook approach to knowledge, thus further frustrating efforts to encourage reading for enjoyment. There's a sense that the curriculum is good just in school, that reading is for grades, and that the written word is a separate entity.

What's a librarian to do? Booktalk the curriculum.

Types of Books

Books play an important role in classroom education because, in addition to providing information, they also stimulate the imagination. Each type of book has different characteristics and therefore requires different booktalking techniques.

Informational books provide an alternative to textbooks. They may be more appropriate to the student's reading level than the text. They may offer different perspectives on the same topic covered in the text, or may cover topics in greater depth than can be done during class time. They may be considered dry fare, so it's up to the booktalker to liven up these treasures and make them seem more appealing.

- Pick out "trivia" facts in an engaging question-and-answer session with the students.
- Poll students about their beliefs about a topic—sharks, for instance—and follow up with titles that relate to that topic. For the shark example, use books by Jacques Cousteau.
- Enlarge photographs from informational books, "crop" them, and produce overhead transparencies for students to interpret. Their discussion can create a nice lead-in for a booktalk.
- Present the book in a mystery format and reveal the solution through booktalking. This technique works especially well with books about inventions and discoveries.
- Play "20 Questions" about a topic and develop a booktalk by giving clues from the book as the game progresses.

- Start a booktalk with a "What if," such as "What if there were no bridges," and build the booktalk around the consequences.
- Bring a prop, such as a model, to attract listeners. [See Bette Ammon and Gale Sherman's article on booktalking with props on page 57 for more information on this topic—**Ed.**]
- Science books are often good grist for "magic" booktalks, because science sometimes looks like magic.

Biographies make learning come alive and help develop a personal connection with the books' subjects. Biographies also affirm each individual's ability to make a difference: a powerful message for youth self-esteem. Biographies are often dramatic stories as well, and appeal to the reader's emotions. Because biographies are "people on paper," booktalkers can use many ways to breathe life into them effectively.

- Dress up as the character and speak of first-hand experiences.
- If the teacher and the librarian team up, one can assume the biographee's persona and the other can conduct an interview. (This takes a lot of preparation, but can be very effective.)
- Dramatize one incident in the person's life.
- Use puppets, such as stick figures, to help students visualize the persons involved.
- Present a group of related people, such as contemporaneous politicians, and compare them. An obvious "panel" would be Abraham Lincoln, Stephen Douglas, Frederick Douglass, and Harriet Beecher Stowe. [Another group could be authors of young adult titles; see the article by Patty Campbell on page 69 for more information on this topic—**Ed.**]
- Hold up pictures of famous and infamous people for students to identify, and do mini-talks on each of them.

Fictional works link the particular to the universal. Historical novels are the classic booktalk tie-in to formal curricula, but contemporary stories and science fiction also provide insights into the human condition. Students identify with the protagonist, imagining themselves in the character's situation. Fiction transcends facts to give a more three-dimensional perspective of the world. Also, students are often impressed when they discover the amount of research that fiction writers must do to present an accurate picture of an era, country, or situation. [Again, see Campbell's article for more information on this topic—**Ed.**]

Fictional booktalks are the norm, so to make them more "curriculum-friendly," try these tactics.

- Ask students what they know about a period in history. Weave the talk about the fictional work around their answers.
- Ask students what they would do in a particular situation, and then tell them how the fictional character acted.
- Dramatize a conflict in the book.
- Have students visualize a particular character, and then lead them through the story from that character's point of view.
- Give several short booktalks about contemporaneous characters—for instance, Civil War figures—or characters from the same historical period but different countries.
- Take a single geographical area, such as France, and give a fictional timeline booktalk.
- Use science fiction stories to forecast the consequences of present trends, such as global warming.

Folktales, myths, and legends offer bigger-than-life perspectives on curricular areas. These "stories of the people" invoke the most universal, basic human values and bridge both time and culture. They are essentially the modern traces of oral tradition and education, and so make for good booktalk material.

- Present one folktale "motif," such as women's search for independence.
- Tell a variety of tales from one geographical area or culture.
- Translate mythology into modern terms.
- Create a modern urban folktale, using books of urban legends and folktales by Daniel Chohen (*The Headless Roommate, Southern Fried Rat, Phone Call from a Ghost*, and others) or the more scholarly volumes by Jan Brunvand (*The Vanishing Hitchhiker, The Choking Doberman*, and *The Mexican Pet*) as booktalked examples.
- Booktalk different creation stories.
- Booktalk different "cause-and-effect," or *pourquoi*, tales that explain how or why things are as they are.
- Show American regionalism through legends of local characters.
- Ask students how they would deal with a conflict. Then booktalk a folktale solution to the problem.

Poetry is an underutilized literary form, especially within the curriculum, yet poems express the most profound details and insights about curricular subjects. In addition,

students respond to poetry's rhythm and pithiness. Some students may be surprised to discover the breadth of subjects that poetry treats: mathematics, sports, transportation, and astronomy, to name a few. A good start when booktalking poetry is to consult *Granger's Guide to Poetry* or some other poetry indexes with a subject approach.

- Intersperse poems between individual booktalks.
- Use poetry as an introductory or ending booktalk.
- Include humorous poetry for comic relief during largely informational booktalks.
- Treat a broad subject, such as war, through dramatic poetry readings.

[For examples of booktalks on poetry, see the section of talks beginning on page 71—**Ed.**]

Fitting Books into the Curriculum

Booktalking can assume different roles relative to the curriculum:

- It can be part of the curriculum
- It can enrich the curriculum
- It can complement the curriculum.

In the first instance, if one uses booktalks as part of the curriculum, they are *integrated within curriculum units*. For instance, if students were studying animals, they might be required to read animal fiction and nonfiction titles. Preferably, students are allowed to choose from a list of possible or suggested readings. Booktalks could then be used to motivate students to read these assignments. If the talks are presented enthusiastically, and if the books themselves are exciting, then the fact that they are required and "good for you" won't spoil students' enjoyment of them. Students might even decide to read more than required!

For this approach to be effective, librarian-teacher coordinated planning is a must. Ideally, the two parties would plan the unit together to choose the titles and decide when booktalks would be done on them. In this way, the librarian can be sure to stock enough copies of titles to satisfy hungry reading appetites, and the timing will maximize the reading results.

The librarian doesn't have to booktalk all the titles. It's fun for students to listen to the librarian and teacher do team booktalks. If good annotated bibliographies are given to students, then they can have an even broader-based selection than the booktalked titles. Instructionally more important, at the end of the unit, students themselves can booktalk any titles that weren't presented at the beginning. They can also compare their literary reading with material learned from the textbook.

When choosing titles, a variety of styles is preferable: informational books, short stories, novels, plays, art, and poetry. For fun, topical riddles and jokes can be an entertaining pastime and booktalk interlude ("A funny thing happened to me on the way to the tar pit . . .").

Booktalks can also *enrich the curriculum*, encouraging worthwhile reading that transcends the classroom experience. Even though *extension* may translate into "extra credit," it can mean freedom from grade constraints and connotations.

Educators are aware of the increasing diversity of students: their backgrounds, their learning styles, their interests and needs. Enrichment booktalks address these varied needs. For the child who has no experience with a different culture, booktalking fictional works helps bridge that student's study of social studies concepts he or she may have trouble understanding. Booktalks extend a curriculum unit's shelf life. When used at the end of a unit, booktalks encourage students to pursue a subject after they've taken their tests. Booktalks then become oral "If you liked . . . then you'll like . . ." pitches for curriculum topics, such as astronomy or Native American studies.

When booktalks present books beyond the assigned readings, teacher-librarian planning need not be so extensive. However, the booktalker should know what general topics are being covered and what texts and readings are being used, so the booktalks will tie in with the students' classroom experiences.

In the third scenario, booktalks *complement the curriculum*. Rather than duplicating the curriculum or working within it, complementary booktalks introduce topics not normally covered by the regular offerings. For instance, if students study mountain and sea life, booktalks might feature desert life. Perhaps the curriculum has no course or unit specifically on careers, but booktalks can provide a means by which to deal with this important issue.

In this situation, the librarian has more autonomy in planning booktalks. Basically, the booktalker needs to know the overall curriculum and its gaps. Also, because the talks are not curriculum-bound, more leeway exists for timing the booktalks. The only disadvantage of such booktalks is that they may seem to exist in limbo, not tied to the rest of the school. Therefore, booktalkers should link talks in some other way: in connection with displays, community events, current news items, or seasonal interests.

Who's Running the Show?

Remember that both school librarians and public librarians can booktalk the curriculum. Although school librarians have built-in advantages in working with teachers, public librarians can work with both school librarians and classroom teachers to expand the curriculum beyond the school walls.

With good communication, these three parties can develop a reading environment that gives the curriculum a life beyond the textbook: a personal meaning that students can take with them into the "Real/Read" world.

Old Reliables

Note: Old Reliables includes works published before 1991.

📖 Ammie, Come Home

Barbara Michaels. Berkeley, 1989. 248p. Paperbound (ISBN 0-425-09949-0) $3.95.
Grades 7–12, Adult. 4Q, 4P.

All Ruth had done was have tea with one of her elderly cousins shortly after she moved to Georgetown, near Washington, D.C. It was a matter of courtesy, nothing more. She couldn't have been more shocked when, years later, she got a letter telling her that the cousin had died and left Ruth her beautiful old Georgetown mansion, stuffed full of antiques. Ruth was surprised, but delighted. She loved old houses, and this one was a real gem. Of course, it was a little big for one person, but after her niece Sara moved in, it didn't seem so empty. In fact, it was practically perfect. The living room was a problem, however. Its lovely antique furniture seemed to resist being rearranged, and there was a strange cold spot near one of the front windows that never warmed up, in spite of the heavy lined drapes at the windows.

Not long after Sara moved in, she began to walk in her sleep—a sleep so deep that Ruth couldn't wake her, a sleep so deep that in the morning Sara had no memory of what had happened the night before. And that wasn't the only thing going on late at night. Both Sara and Ruth heard a neighbor calling a pet named Sammie, calling over and over and over. It wasn't until they discovered that none of the neighbors' pets were named Sammie that Ruth and Sara began to wonder just exactly what was going on. They had joked about old Cousin Hattie haunting the house—but now they began to wonder if it was no joke at all. And the deeper they dug into the family past, the more dangerous it became for Sara and everyone she loved.

—Marijo Duncan
Phoenix Public Library, Phoenix, AZ

📖 And This Is Laura

Ellen Conford. Little, Brown, 1977, 1992.
179p. Paperbound (ISBN 0-316-15354-0)
$4.95. **Grades 5–8. 3Q, 4P.**

This is Laura's sister, Jill, who's an actress. This is Laura's brother, Douglas, who plays the piano and composes music. This is Laura's other brother, Dennis, who recites TV commercials from memory. And this is Laura. She's 12.

That's all. She doesn't have any special talents, doesn't play any musical instruments, hasn't gotten any wonderful awards. More than anything else in the world, Laura wants to have some special talent that would make her fit in with her super-talented family.

Then one night, at dinner, she discovers what her special talent is—she's psychic. She has visions, and they come true. She can predict the future—and she's good at it. At first, it's wonderful, because everyone wants to know what their future will be. But then dark visions start coming, and one of them is about her brother Dennis. Should she tell someone? Should she just stop using the gift, so she won't see any more bad things? But the gift is her only talent. Or is it?

—Colleen Smith
Town of Haldimand Public Libraries,
Caledonia, Ontario, Canada

📖 Angel Dust Blues

Todd Strasser. Dell, 1981. 208p. Paperbound
(ISBN 0-440-90156-2) $2.95. **Grades 9–12.
4Q, 3P.**

Alex is a high school senior living in New York City. You may or may not have a lot in common with him. To start with, he's rich; he has all the money he needs. Second, he gets good grades, almost straight As. He's popular, has lots of friends, and is a pretty good athlete—in fact, his life seems too good to be true. He doesn't even have to hassle with his parents—they live in Florida. He has the whole house to himself.

What would you do in a situation like that? What about party? That's what everyone expects Alex to do. In fact, everyone seems to have an idea about what Alex should be doing: his teachers, his parents, their stuffy friends, even his own friends—everyone, it seems, except Alex himself. Sometimes he feels like he's listening to 10 radio stations at once, with all the different voices he hears telling him what's expected of him.

That's when he meets Michael, who's his exact opposite. Alex is rich; Michael is working-class. Alex gets good grades; Michael is a burnout. But opposites frequently attract, and soon these two people who have nothing in common are close friends. In fact, they're more than just friends—they're business partners, salesmen working on their high school campus.

But they aren't selling Avon products—they're selling drugs. Michael had been small time, just selling joints in the locker room, but with Alex's money, they get into cocaine and are soon the biggest dealers in school. Finally, Alex thinks he knows who he is and what he wants.

Just about then, Alex meets Ellen. Suddenly, selling drugs isn't as glamorous as it had seemed. It's dangerous and it's wrong, and Alex decides he wants out—but not until after he and Michael set up one last deal. They take all the money they've earned and buy a big score of angel dust. Then Michael disappears, and Alex has no idea how to find him. Three days later, there's a knock on the door. It's the police, and they've come to arrest him for selling drugs.

"Come on, Alex, we know you sell drugs at school."

"Me? No way. You've got the wrong person."

"We know that your buddy Michael is behind it. Why don't you tell us where he is?"

"I don't know where he is."

"Don't protect him, he's scum."

"He's my best friend, not scum, but I still don't know where he is."

"Listen, Alex, if we can't find Michael, we're going to arrest you. You can kiss your nice house, your nice car, your nice girlfriend, and your nice future goodbye. Here's my card. Think about it."

Alex does think about it, while a couple of days go by. Then Alex hears a noise in the garage and goes to investigate. He finds Michael lying on the floor, bloody and beaten up, helpless as a baby. And Michael says, "Alex, you gotta help me. You're my best friend. You're the only person I trust."

Is it ever right to betray your best friend, even if it's to help you lose the *Angel Dust Blues*?

—Patrick Jones
Allen County Public Library, Fort Wayne, IN

📖 Are You in the House Alone?

Richard Peck. Dell, 1977. 176p. Paperbound (ISBN 0-440-90227-4) $3.50. Viking, 1976. 176p. Hardbound (ISBN 0-670-13241-1) $15.00. **Grades 9–12. 3Q, 2P.**

Gail is in awe of the power the Lawver family seems to have in her hometown. They're rich and powerful and their name seems to be on everything. Sometimes it seems like the town should be called Lawverville. But Gail isn't a part of Phil Lawver's crowd. She goes with Steve Pastorini, even though her parents don't approve of him. They think she could do better than Steve, maybe even date someone like Phil Lawver. But Gail and Steve are in love, and she refuses to give him up to please her parents. They

don't see each other as much as they'd like to, though, because they both work.

Gail really enjoyed baby-sitting, until the notes and the phone calls started. She finds the notes in her locker at school, and they say things like: "You know you want it. You'll get it. And you won't have long to wait." The phone calls come when she's baby-sitting, a strange voice whispering to her, "Are you in the house alone?" Suddenly, staying alone in a strange house at night isn't as easy as it used to be. Now the dark is threatening and dangerous. Then one night, shortly after Gail has slammed the phone down on yet another of the phone calls, she hears a knock on the door. She opens it, expecting to see Steve, but instead it's Phil Lawver outside. He asks if he can come in and use the phone. Gail lets him in and walks away to give him some privacy. But the next thing she hears is the voice she's been hearing over the phone, "Are you in the house alone?" Only this time—she isn't.

—Patrick Jones
Allen County Public Library, Fort Wayne, IN

📖 Buck

Tamela Larimer. Avon, 1986. 176p. Paperbound (ISBN 0-380-75172-0) $2.50. **Grades 9–12. 4Q, 4P.**

Has a friend of yours, maybe even your best friend, ever come up to you and said, "Do you want to know a secret? Promise not to tell, no matter what?" That's how this book gets started.

Buck's run away from home. He's been on the road for days, and he's out of food, out of money, out of ideas, and just about out of hope. When he sees a kid his own age, he hides in the kid's car, so when Rich gets in, he sees Buck for the first time. But instead of being scared or mad, Rich is curious. They start talking and hit it off immediately. Although Rich is popular at school, he doesn't really have a best friend, and Buck is desperate. Buck tells Rich all about running away, and then he says, "I'm going to tell you a secret. I'm going to tell you the real reason I ran away, but you have to promise me you won't tell anyone, ever, for any reason."

"Okay, I promise."

"No, you have to swear to me you'll never tell."

"I swear." And Buck tells Rich his secret.

Buck ends up moving in with Rich and his family. When school starts that year, Rich introduces Buck to all his friends at school, most of them part of the popular athlete crowd. Rich tells Buck only one thing about how to get along in school. He warns him to avoid this kid named Buzz, who's the leader of the burnout kids.

So what's one of the first things Buck does? He messes with Buzz. But instead of being mad, Buzz is impressed, and tells all the other burnouts that Buck is okay and to watch out for him. That means Buck has made friends in both of the big cliques at school. In addition, most of the teachers like him, and a lot of girls have crushes on him. It's not long before Buck is the most popular guy in school.

Only one person at school doesn't like Buck. His name is Tony, and he *hates* Buck. Tony was the most popular guy in school until Buck arrived. Now he's lost his starting place on the football team and his girlfriend. When Buck shows up at an after-game party with Tony's ex-girlfriend, Tony loses it. He waits for his chance and then jumps Buck. Just when it looks like Tony's going to win, Buzz and a bunch of burnouts show up and beat Tony up so badly that he ends up in the hospital.

Now Rich is in a fix. He doesn't know whether he should be loyal to his old friend Tony or his new friend Buck. He kind of likes being Buck's friend—it's fun being the best friend of the most popular kid in school. He starts feeling more popular, and decides to ask out a girl he's liked for a long time. But she refuses to go with him, and when he pushes her for an answer, she tells him it's because she likes Buck.

Well, that makes Rich's decision about loyalty easy, and he and Tony get together. They're sitting around feeling angry and getting drunk. Tony says, "I really want to get back at Buck. I don't want to hurt him physically, but I really want to make him suffer."

"You want people to hate him?" Rich asks.

"You bet! I want people to hate him as much as I do. I want him to be the most unpopular kid in school."

For a moment there's silence. Rich opens another beer and passes it to Tony. Then he says, "Hey, Tony, you want to know a secret?"

—Patrick Jones
Allen County Public Library, Fort Wayne, IN

📖 Chain Letter

Christopher Pike. Avon, 1986. 192p. Paperbound (ISBN 0-380-89968-X) $3.50. **Grades 7–12. 4Q, 4P.**

When they hit him, they were sure he was dead. They were going so fast and hit him so hard, they were sure he was dead. When they got out of the car to look at the body, they were sure he was dead. They put the body in the trunk and drove to an open field. They didn't have a shovel, so they used their hands. The ground was hard, so the grave was shallow. One of them said a quick prayer and they left the grave. It was only after the letter came that one of them dared to say out loud: "How can we be *sure* he was dead?"

The letter said, "My dear friend. You do not know me, but I know you. Since you first breathed in this world, I have watched you. The hopes you have wished, the sins you have committed. I know them all. I am the Observer. I am also the Punisher. The time has come for your punishment."

And then there was a list of their names: Fran, Kipp, Brenda, Neil, Joan, Tony, and Alison. Everyone who had been in the car that night—they were all on the list. The letter also said that each one of them would have to perform a small service, or else they would be hurt. And the letter was signed "Your Caretaker."

Fran's task was simple: replace the school mascot. Kipp's was a little harder: the straight-A student was told to flunk a test. Brenda was told to tell off a teacher in front of everyone, and Neil was told to get sick in class. Joan was a fashion plate. She really cared about how she looked and what she wore. She spent hours getting ready for school every morning. The Caretaker told her to go to school dressed like Bozo the Clown. She refused, just like Kipp, and for a while nothing happened. Then one night the window of her bedroom seemed to explode. She got up and started walking toward it. As she walked, she heard a strange crunching sound under her bare feet. Her first thought was broken glass, but while it hurt her feet, whatever she was walking on didn't cut them. She walked toward the window. Crunch crunch. She leaned over the lamp, turned it on, and screamed. She had not been walking on broken glass, but on the cockroaches that covered her floor like a carpet. Tony is told to lose a track meet and Alison is told to mess up in the school play. After Joan's experience, they didn't dare disobey.

Now what, they wondered. What more could he force them to do? Then The Caretaker's second letter arrived, and they all knew that neither they nor their secret were safe. Suddenly, they realized that they would have to pull together, because every chain has its weakest link. When that link broke, the chain broke. And if their chain broke, some people were going to get hurt—hurt bad.

They thought about the accident. They thought about the man. They thought about the grave. They thought about that question, "How do we *know* he was dead?" And they thought about The Caretaker, because if they couldn't stop him, by the time he was through, they'd all be dead, no questions asked.

—Patrick Jones
Allen County Public Library, Fort Wayne, IN

📖 Dealing with Dragons

Patricia C. Wrede. Scholastic, 1992. 212p. Paperbound (ISBN 0-590-45722-5) $3.25. Harcourt Brace Jovanovich, 1990. 212p. Hardbound (ISBN 0-152-22900-0) $15.95. **Grades 5–12, adults. 4Q, 3P.**

Cimorene's parents, the King and Queen, always tried to be good parents. They raised their first six daughters to be perfectly proper princesses. They all have long, golden hair and sweet dispositions, and are interested in dancing, embroidery, drawing, and etiquette. Then there's the seventh daughter, Cimorene, the royal nightmare.

To begin with, she doesn't have the requisite princess hair. Her hair is jet black and she wears it in a braid. Plus, she's interested in entirely improper things, like fencing, magic, and economics. And as for a sweet disposition, when people are being polite, they just say she's strong-minded. When they are annoyed with her, which is most of the time, they say she's stubborn as a pig.

So it's no surprise that when Cimorene's parents announce her upcoming marriage to a local prince, she flatly refuses. Prince Therandil is golden-haired and blue-eyed, but unfortunately doesn't have much in the way of brains. As Cimorene says, "He has no sense of humor; he isn't intelligent; he can't talk about anything except tourneys; and half of what he does say he gets wrong."

When Cimorene's parents refuse to humor her this time, she does what any other self-respecting princess would do—she volunteers to be a captive princess of the dragons. And since she can cook a mean cherries jubilee and has a passing knowledge of Latin, one of the oldest and wisest of the dragons takes her on as his servant, in spite of the other dragons' desire to eat her now and get it over with. Cimorene soon discovers that being a dragon's captive princess can be a surprisingly enjoyable occupation.

Now her only problem is how to deal with Prince Therandil, who has developed the increasingly annoying habit of trying to rescue her every couple of days. What's a princess to do?

—Becky Shulz
Bedford Public Library, Bedford, NH

📖 Devil's Race

Avi. Avon, 1987. 128p. Paperbound (ISBN 0-380- 70406-4) $2.95. HarperCollins, 1984. 160p. Hardbound (ISBN 0-397-32094-9) $12.95. **Grades 7–8. 3Q, 3P.**

Have you ever gotten a homework assignment that you just couldn't do, so you kept putting it off and putting it off, hoping that somehow you won't have to do it after all? That's the problem John Proud is having. He's a good student, but he just can't do the family history report he's supposed to do. But what John Proud doesn't realize is that his family history is nothing to be proud of. Instead of writing about it, he should be trying to forget about it.

But John finally gets down to it, and discovers that his great-great-great-grandfather, also named John Proud, was hanged in 1854. His crime? The townspeople said he was a demon—and they were right. Just before they hanged him, John Proud asked to say his last words, and then proceeded to curse the town, proclaim that he was indeed a demon, and swear that although they could hang him, they would never be rid of him. *That* is John Proud's family history!

Curious to find out more about this demon who shared his name, John sets off to find his grave. What a feeling it must have been for him to stand in front of the gravestone and see his own name written there—John Proud RIP. He just stands there and stares at it for a long time. He leaves, but returns only a moment later. When he returns, he senses right away that something is different, that something is wrong. Then he sees the boy about his own age sitting on top of the gravestone. "Hello, John," the boy says. "My name is John Proud. The first John Proud." The demon from 1854 has come back to haunt him. John Proud's family history has come to life, and the *Devil's Race* is on.

—Patrick Jones
Allen County Public Library, Fort Wayne, IN

📖 Discontinued

Julian Thompson. Scholastic, 1987. 304p. Paperbound (ISBN 0-590-42464-5) $3.50. Scholastic, 1986. 304p. Hardbound (ISBN 0-590-3321-6) $12.95. **Grades 9–12. 3Q, 2P.**

[This talk should be done at a rapid-fire pace—**PJ.**]

THIS IS NOT A BOOK ABOUT BASKETBALL. I could see how you might think this is about basketball, but THIS IS NOT A BOOK ABOUT BASKETBALL. Sure, it begins with our hero Duncan playing a game of basketball, but trust me on this one—THIS IS NOT A BOOK ABOUT BASKETBALL. Even though our hero Duncan does play on his high school basketball team, THIS IS NOT A BOOK ABOUT BASKETBALL. Oh, I forgot to mention that this is a state championship high school basketball team our hero plays on, but that really isn't important, because THIS IS NOT A BOOK ABOUT BASKETBALL. So, Duncan is walking home from school after playing a game of basketball, and the entire time he is dribbling a basketball, but THIS IS NOT A BOOK ABOUT BASKETBALL. And when he gets about two blocks from home, he sees his mother and his brother. This is your clue that THIS IS NOT A BOOK ABOUT BAS-

KETBALL, because his mother doesn't play basketball. But she does spend a lot of time going shopping, and this is what she's about to do when Duncan sees her and his brother get into the family car. But when she turns the key, the bomb planted in the car blows up, and Duncan sees his mother and his little brother blown up with it, and there's absolutely nothing he can do, because it's over before he realizes what's happening. And that's why THIS IS NOT A BOOK ABOUT BASKETBALL, because it's a book about who planted the bomb, and why, and what Duncan is going to do about it.

—*Patrick Jones*
Allen County Public Library, Fort Wayne, IN

📖 Dreamland Lake

Richard Peck. Dell, 1982, 1992. 128p. Paperbound (ISBN 0-440-92079-5) $3.25. Holt, 1973; Peter Smith, 1992. 150p. Hardbound (ISBN 0-8446-6542-8) $16.00. **Grades 5–8. 3Q, 2P.**

B rian and Flip suffer from one of the worst diseases known to man. It usually lasts only a year, but it is the worst year you can possibly imagine. It makes people ignore you. Your friends won't talk to you and you feel almost totally alone. Your body changes and everything else seems different too. You always get over it, but you never forget it. It is the disease everyone hates to have. It is the disease known as seventh grade.

Brian and Flip are nobodies at their school, just two seventh-grade geeks that teachers ignore and older kids beat up on. Nobodies until the day they find the dead body at Dreamland Lake. It was a man's body and they found it in the weeds at the woodsy end of Dreamland Lake. After they find the body, they go from being nobodies to being big-time celebrities. Teachers pay attention to them, they don't get beat up as often, and they get their names and faces on the radio, on TV, and in the newspaper. Seventh-grade celebrities—but not for long. As soon as the big news becomes old news, they're just seventh graders again.

But Brian likes being a celebrity, and figures that if they got so popular from just finding the body, they'll be even bigger celebrities if they discover how it got there. So Brian and Flip set out to solve the mystery of the dead body. However, when they return to Dreamland Lake, two strange things happen. First, they notice swastikas carved into the trees and bridges near the lake. Then they find an old deserted building, and inside, more swastikas and a table with black candle wax on it. It looks like it could be an altar—but why? But even that isn't as strange as the second thing that happens. They take pictures of the area, and when they're developed, there's a face in the background. At first they think it's a ghost, but then they realize it's something even worse. It's Elvan.

Elvan is another seventh grader, a fat, ugly, greasy kid that everyone hates. What is he doing in their pictures? What is he doing at Dreamland Lake? Brian and Flip decide to trick him to find out what's going on. They're sure that if they just ask him, he'll lie. Elvan doesn't have any friends, and so Brian and Flip pretend to make friends with him. That way, when they ask him what he was doing at Dreamland Lake, he won't be suspicious. Then one day Elvan asks them over to his house so he can show them something. They go down to the basement, where Elvan unlocks the door to his room. But when Brian and Flip step inside, they see a sight that's all too familiar, one that they never expected to see. The room is decorated all over with swastikas. What does Elvan have to do with the body? Why are his room and an old deserted building both covered with swastikas? The answer to those questions is the solution to the mystery of *Dreamland Lake*.

—*Patrick Jones*
Allen County Public Library, Fort Wayne, IN

📖 Fall of the Flamingo Circus

Kate Rigby. Random House, 1990. 213p. Hardbound (ISBN 0-394-58356-6) $16.95. **Grades 9–12, adults. 3Q, 1P.**

D o you know anyone who's really strange? I don't mean your brother with his Ninja Turtles fetish, or your cousin who won't eat meat and speaks in rhyme, or even the jock down the street who thinks his body is a temple. I mean someone who seems to be completely out of it, someone whose every act, every word, even every article of clothing seems designed to make people uncomfortable, to attract attention while making absolutely sure that no one, but no one, gets too close. Don't know anyone quite like that? Well, meet Lauren Schanzer.

Lauren's from Northern England, her family's poor, there are lots of kids, her father drinks and hits, her real mother left long ago, and her stepmother can't cope with the kids and won't stand up to her husband. Lauren is smart enough, but the way her family lives and the way she speaks make her an outcast from the middle class, with its proper upbringing and proper accents.

Not wanting to belong to the lower class where her accent and home life have sentenced her, and rejected by the middle class where she would like to belong, Lauren is ready for change, a chance to show the world, defy convention in every way. Punk is the way she chooses. And I don't mean torn designer jeans and pressed rock star t-shirts, I mean the real thing: ragged clothes, dead-white make-up, wildly spiked and colored hair, chains and pins for jewelry, and a damn-your-eyes attitude. It's ugly, scary, rude, and outrageous, a way to say to everyone else, "I'm gonna do and say and be what I want to, and what the hell are you gonna do about it?"

Lauren is really strange. But the things that hurt her, the things she cares about, the things she does or doesn't understand about herself—I feel them . . . I understand them, and maybe you will, too. And that makes me feel strange, I mean, *really* strange.

[This title includes a lot of British slang, which may make the book less accessible for American teenagers. However, it has enough good things to say that I feel it should be considered for large collections in spite of it— **RM**]

—*Rene Mandel*
Framington, MA

Felicia the Critic

Ellen Conford. Illustrated by Arvis L. Stewart. Little, Brown, 1973, 1992. 137p. Paperbound (ISBN 0-316-15358-3) $4.95. Little Brown, 1973. 145p. Hardbound (ISBN 0-316-15295-1) $13.95. **Grades 3–6. 3Q, 3P.**

When Felicia Kershenbaum sees someone doing something that's wrong, she thinks it's her job to tell them about it. And she sees a lot of people doing a lot of things wrong! But not everyone likes being told about what they're doing wrong, especially Felicia's friends and family, who seem to do more things wrong than anyone else.

Finally Felicia's mother steps in and explains the difference between destructive and constructive criticism. Felicia thinks she understands, but she's sure that some criticism must be okay, because there are people who make their living being critics. And Felicia is so good at criticism that she decides that she'll become a critic—starting now! So instead of saying negative things to people, Felicia begins to make lists of what people can do to improve themselves. She makes one for the crossing guard, telling him how to direct traffic better; one for her sister Marilyn, offering suggestions for prettier names; and one for her aunt, the author, telling her all the things Felicia didn't like about her new children's book.

But even though Felicia means well and is just trying to help, people still don't like her criticism. In fact, they hate it. Some of her friends say they won't let her into their club unless she promises never to criticize anything again. Can she do it? What if she sees someone making a really big mistake? Should she stay quiet and keep her friends and stay in the club, or should she let someone know about their big mistake, and get kicked out?

—*Colleen Smith*
Town of Haldimand Public Libraries, Caledonia, Ontario, Canada

Gentlehands

M. E. Kerr. HarperCollins, 1980. 192p. Paperbound (ISBN 0-06-447067-9) $3.95. HarperCollins, 1978. 212p. Hardbound (ISBN 0-06-023177-7) $16.95. **Grades 7–12. 4Q, 2P.**

All Buddy wanted to do was impress Skye Pennington. She was beautiful, rich, and the love of his life. He couldn't impress her the way she impressed him, taking him to the country club, driving around in a fancy car, or meeting lots of her rich friends and relatives. Buddy didn't have anything or anyone like that, except his grandfather. Grandfather Tinker was an odd sort of fellow. He wasn't real close to Buddy or anyone else in his family. He was a recluse who spent most of his time in a large house upstate. Buddy didn't even know that much about him. He knew that Grandfather Tinker had come from Germany after World War II, knew that he had money, and knew that he had class, so he figured that Grandfather Tinker would be just the person to impress Skye Pennington.

And it worked. She was impressed. The way Grandfather talked, the wine he drank, the opera he listened to, and the way his house was decorated. Skye was impressed, and Buddy had his grandfather to thank. But as he got to know his grandfather better, Buddy also got more curious about him, just as some other people were. People like Mr. De Lucca, who didn't want to know about Grandfather Tinker's present, but about his past. Not about who he is, but about who he was. And when De Lucca discovers the truth about Grandfather Tinker's past, and shares it with Buddy, Buddy refuses to believe it.

What would you do if you found out that a person you loved had done terrible things that you hated? Was his grandfather the monster De Lucca said he was, or was he the gentle man Buddy had come to know and love? How could he have committed such unspeakable crimes with such *Gentlehands*?

—*Patrick Jones*
Allen County Public Library, Fort Wayne, IN

Living with a Parent Who Drinks Too Much

Judith S. Sexias. Nonfiction. Beech Tree Books, 1979, 1991. 116p. Paperbound (ISBN 0-688-10493-2) $3.25. **Grades 5–8. 4Q, 1P.**

Living with a Parent Who Takes Drugs

Judith S. Sexias. Nonfiction. Beech Tree Books, 1989, 1991. 102p. Paperbound (ISBN 0-688-10492-4) $3.25. **Grades 5–8. 4Q, 1P.**

Amy knew that her home was not like the homes her friends had. In fact, none of her friends had ever seen her home—she knew better than to invite anyone to her home. She didn't want the outside world to know what went on in her home. She was ashamed of everything and everyone in it, including her three younger sisters.

To escape from the chaos, she retreated to her room and to her "nest," a fuzzy cover on her bed that she could shape into a nestlike circle. From there she could look out her window at the birds flying free in the sky. It was terribly lonely, and many times she was terrified by the quarreling and fighting that she could hear outside her closed door. She worried about what was happening and feared that it was somehow all her fault.

Finally, Amy learned that her mother was an alcoholic. That was the reason for the way her parents acted—it didn't have anything to do with Amy at all. Amy even wrote a note to herself to remind her: "My mother is an alcoholic. She is sick."

Find out how Amy learned to cope with her life, and how to find friends and help, so she didn't have to stay curled up in her nest every day.

Jason, a junior high student, was ashamed of his parents, too, and didn't know what to do about it. Finally, he told his school counselor, and she was able to help him understand how to live with two parents who took drugs.

Living with a parent who drinks or takes drugs isn't fun and it isn't easy. But you aren't as alone as you might feel, and there are ways to help you deal with the situation. Let the kids in these books show you how.

—*Sharon Thomas*
Goddard ILC/JH Library, Goddard, KS

📖 Lupita Mañana

Patricia Beatty. Beech Tree Books, 1992. 190p. Paperbound (ISBN 0-688-11497-0) $4.95. William Morrow, 1981. 192p. Hardbound (ISBN 0-688-00359-1) $12.95. **Grades 5-8. 4Q, 2P.**

Thirteen-year-old Lupita Torres is called Lupita Mañana, because even though she is one of six children of a poor Mexican fisherman, she believes that life will be better *mañana*—tomorrow. But when her father drowns during a storm at sea, even Lupita finds it hard to believe in a better tomorrow. Her mother is a hotel maid, and can't earn enough money to support all of her children. The only way for them to survive is to send Lupita and Salvador, the two oldest, across the border to their Aunt Consuelo in California. Once in the United States, they can earn enough money to live on and still send some home to

their mother. But since they have no skills or money, and can't speak English, the two teenagers have to sneak across the border, hoping to avoid the border police who would send them back to Mexico or to jail if they are captured.

Life in the United States isn't what Lupita had hoped for. The only job she can find is working in the fields. Salvador quickly makes flashy new Mexican-American friends, and forgets about his little sister and his other obligations. Aunt Consuelo's home is not the safe refuge Lupita had hoped for, either, and she soon realizes that without English and without an education, she will spend all her mañanas in poverty.

—*Maureen Whalen*
Rochester Public Library, Rochester, NY

📖 The Midnight Horse

Sid Fleischman. Illustrated by Peter Sis. Dell, 1992. 84p. Paperbound (ISBN 0-440-40614-5) $3.50. Greenwillow, 1990. 84p. Hardbound (ISBN 0-688-09441-4) $13.00. **Grades 3–6. 3Q, 3P.**

Have you ever heard of the Great Chaffalo and his world-famous horse trick? Well, I hadn't either, until I traveled to Cricklewood to see if my great-uncle would take me in. The Red Raven Inn in Cricklewood even has an autographed poster of the Great Chaffalo himself.

Chaffalo was a tall man with a broad red sash across his chest and an equally broad smile on his face. He was born in Cricklewood, but traveled the world performing his act. He was given a beautiful chiming watch by the King of Prussia. He always came back here, though, to rest after his travels, in the summer house he had built.

He was a great magician, and I'd heard that he'd even pinched a Chinese coin off a young boy's nose! And his most famous trick of all was his horse trick. He could snap his fingers and turn a pile of straw into a horse. But even though he had an exciting life, the great Chaffalo didn't live long. He was shot and went to an early grave. Only his ghost lives in the old summer house now. At least, I hope it does—I'm going to need some help real soon.

You see, my great-uncle is an old grouch. He wouldn't take me in, and now he's trying to take my inheritance away from me, and the Red Raven Inn away from Miss Sally. We could really use some help, but I'm not sure what the Great Chaffalo and his horse can do now—they're only ghosts. Can a ghost still do magic?

—*C. Allen Nichols*
Rocky River Public Library, Rocky River, OH

📖 Monkey See, Monkey Do

Barthe deClements. Dell, 1992. 146p. Paperbound (ISBN 0-440-10675-7) $3.50. Delacorte, 1990. 146p. Hardbound (ISBN 0-385-30158-8) $13.95. **Grades 3–6. 3Q, 3P.**

Jerry reached for the branch to pretend to fall from the tree house, but the branch really broke, and he crashed to the ground, spraining his wrist. A real fall was even better than a fake one, though, because his dad didn't go to the mall with Rattler and Louie. He took Jerry to the emergency room instead. You see, Jerry's dad was back home after spending two years in prison, and he wasn't supposed to associate with ex-cons, especially when the reason they were going to the mall was to hotwire cars! When Jerry couldn't talk his dad out of going, faking a fall from the tree house seemed to be the only solution. But it didn't work. Rattler and Louie took Jerry's mom's car to the mall anyway. They got caught stealing cars, and the police came to pick up Jerry's dad later.

Jerry's dad was in prison for 90 days this time, but when he got out he promised to go straight. He did for a while, and even had a job, until he got fired. That's why he wasn't working and why Jerry called him when the teacher needed one more parent to go on the field trip with them. The field trip was great, until they stopped for ice cream on the way home and Jerry's dad got in trouble again. Will Jerry ever have a happy home? Will his dad ever be able to stay out of trouble? And what about the decision Jerry's mom made the last time his dad was in prison? Is there anything Jerry can do to help?

—*Dorothy Davidson*
Allie Ward Elementary School, Abilene, TX

📖 The Mouse Rap

Walter Dean Myers. HarperCollins, 1992. 186p. Paperbound (ISBN 0-06-440356-4) $3.95. HarperCollins, 1989. 192p. Hardbound (ISBN 0-06-024343-0) $14.00. **Grades 5–8. 2Q, 2P.**

Come and listen to my story 'bout a boy named Mouse
Lookin' for some loot in a deserted gangster house.
Has a bunch of friends helpin' look for the place,
There's Sheri, and Bev, and a guy named Ace,
Plus an old gangster man, used to live on the run,
And a little bitty kid who likes to pack a gun.
In addition to the search, most of this group
Likes to spend the summer playin' some hoop,

Singin' and dancin' and doin' a show,
Gettin' into trouble and a whole lot mo'.
To find out what happens—if they find that treasure
Read *The Mouse Rap*—it'll give you pleasure.

—*Jeff Blair*
South Olathe High School, Olathe, KS

📖 Muggie Maggie

Beverly Cleary. Illustrated by Kay Life. Avon, 1991. 80p. Paperbound (ISBN 0-380-7187-0) $3.50. Morrow, 1990. 70p. Hardbound (ISBN 0-688-08553-9) $13.95. **Grades 3–4. 4Q, 3P.**

Mrs. Leeper, Maggie's new teacher, says everyone is going to have a good time in third grade, but Maggie doesn't think so, not when they have to learn cursive writing! What's wrong with printing, anyway, or using the computer? Who needs all those loops and squiggles? So Maggie decides she just won't learn it; she'll draw roller coasters instead. But she does learn about closed loops and straight letters, and one day she decides to try writing her name. But it comes out looking like *Muggie* instead of *Maggie*, and all the kids tease her about not learning to write. Then Mrs. Leeper selects Maggie as the message monitor, and asks her to take a message to the principal and wait for an answer. Maggie takes a tiny peek at the message on her way to the office. But she can't read it because it's in cursive. On her way back, she peeks at the answer and recognizes her name. What has she done to make the principal write a note with her name in it? But Maggie doesn't have time to worry, because she's being kept busy taking messages all over the school, messages that she can't read, except for her own name. That's when Maggie decides it's time she learns how to read and write cursive, so she can find out why her name is in all those messages.

—*Colleen Smith*
Town of Haldimand Public Libraries, Caledonia, Ontario, Canada

📖 My Darling, My Hamburger

Paul Zindel. Bantam, 1984. 176p. Paperbound (ISBN 0-553-27324-8) $3.50. HarperCollins, 1969. 176p. Hardbound (ISBN 0-06-026824-7) $12.95. **Grades 7–12. 3Q, 3P.**

A long time ago, back in the 1960s, there weren't lots of books written for teenagers like there are now. There were a few, but they weren't all that good. The people that wrote them didn't seem to have any idea what it was like to be a teenager. The books were all very "well, children, just drink your milk, say your prayers, take your vitamins, obey your teachers and your parents, and everything will be just hunky dory." Well, we all know that being 14 is a lot tougher than that. So does Paul Zindel. In the late 60s he started writing books about what it was really like to be a teenager. This is one of his books, *My Darling, My Hamburger*.

Pretty weird title? Well, before I tell you about the title, let me tell you about some of the people in this book. It's basically a romance between Liz and Sean and between Dennis and Maggie. But none of them are exactly average. Sean is really smart at math. He also likes to think about killing himself. So he combines his two main interests by figuring out complex mathematical formulas estimating how large a hole he can blow in his head with any kind of gun. Liz is a little bit less tense—in fact, she's one of the class clowns. Her idea of a joke is to change the caption in the yearbook for the girl voted "most likely to succeed" to "girl most likely for boys to succeed with." Maggie and Dennis aren't the kind of couple you'd run into just any day either. Maggie says that Dennis's face looks like an undernourished zucchini, and Dennis says that her ears are too small. Sweet Valley High this is not.

So you can read this as a romance. Or you can read it as a book about growing up in the 60s. Or you can read it as a book about being a senior in high school. Or you can read it as a book about how hard it is to be a teenager. Or you can read it because you like books that make fun of all the stupid things that teachers, parents, and other adults say.

And speaking of stupid things, remember the title? *My Darling, My Hamburger*—what does that mean? Well, during biology Miss Fanuzzi is giving her yearly lecture on human sexual reproduction. She hates to stand up in front of a class of teenagers and talk about sex, so she races through the lecture and then makes the mistake of saying, "Any questions?" She doesn't expect to get any, but she does.

"I have a question about human sexual reproduction."

"Yes," said Miss Fanuzzi, turning red.

"What do you do when a boy wants to go all the way?"

Miss Fanuzzi didn't say anything for a few seconds. Then in a very tense voice she said, "You should stop whatever you are doing and go out and get a hamburger."

But the problem Liz and Sean have is this—they don't live near a Wendy's, a McDonalds, or even a Burger King.

—*Patrick Jones*
Allen County Public Library, Fort Wayne, IN

📖 Mystery Walk

Robert McCammon. Ballantine, 1989. 419p. Paperbound (ISBN 0-345-31514-6) $4.95. **Grades 9–12, adults. 4Q, 4P.**

Ten-year-old Billy Creekmore grew up in the South, and grew up poor. His father worked very hard to put food on the table. His mother worked very hard, too, but she only worked in the house. She didn't go into town much any more, not after what had happened just before Billy was born. The townspeople let her alone too. But Billy has friends in town, and his best friend is Will Booker. That is, until Mr. Booker killed Will, his sister, his mother, and then himself. They found the little girl and her mother right away, but they couldn't find Will's body. But Billy found him. One day he was walking past the Booker house, the Death House it was called now, and he heard someone calling to him. The voice kept calling until it led Billy down to the cellar where the winter supply of coal was stored. In the coal pile, the voice said. In the coal pile. In the coal pile. Over and over the voice talked to Billy, silently, in his own head. That's how Billy discovered that he had inherited his mother's ability to set the dead to rest and to take away their pain.

But Billy isn't the only boy growing up in the South with unusual powers. Little Wayne Faulkner is 10 years old, too, the son of the South's best-loved evangelist. And while Billy can give the dead peace, Little Wayne can heal the living. He travels around the countryside healing the sick and maimed in the name of the Lord.

And Billy's and Wayne's powers have been noticed by someone who does not wish them well. It is an entity called the Shape Changer, and it can look like anything or anybody. Its goal in life, if it has a life, is to kill both Billy and Wayne, and snuff out their powers forever.

—*Marijo Duncan*
Phoenix Public Library, Phoenix, AZ

📖 The Pit

Ann Cheetham. Holt, 1990. 154p. Hardcover (ISBN 0-8050-1142-0) $14.95. **Grades 5–6. 4Q, 3P.**

The sound of the crying woman was clearer now. Oliver's scalp tingled and his stomach lurched. He found himself gliding sideways toward the crack opening like a huge mouth in the cellar wall. A roaring blackness swept out of the crack, surrounding Oliver, choking him and swallowing him up.

Oliver had always liked horrible, grisly things. He would sneak horror comics and creepy books up to his attic room. He had to smuggle them in because his mother disapproved of that sort of thing. Lately, Oliver had been hanging around the excavation site near his house. The site was right next to the old graveyard, and Oliver hoped that maybe the machines would disturb an old grave. That would be interesting.

Well, something had been disturbed, all right. Oliver's friend Ted, who worked on the demolition site, encountered it first. Oliver had seen Ted running blindly down the street, a moaning, sobbing noise like the helpless cry of a child coming from his throat. Looking at Ted, Oliver had felt the darkness for the first time. Ted had not returned to the pit, but the work went on. Small things were found. Oliver was given a strange black stone with nearly invisible writing scratched on it and a pair of almost unrecognizable tiny shoes. And the work trucks rumbling down the road had brought the crack in the wall. Oliver's cellar was now open to the earth of the graveyard. The strange thing was, as much as Oliver feared the darkness, he was also drawn to it. And so he let himself go into the blackness.

In the pit, Oliver found more horror than he could ever have imagined. What does he find? Step into the pit with him and find out.

—*Julie Bray*
Jasper County Public Library, Rensselaer, IN

Raising the Stones

Sheri S. Tepper. Doubleday, 1990. 453p. Hardbound (ISBN 0-385-41510-9) $19.95. **Grades 9–12, adult. 4Q, 4P.**

Maire Manone, the Voice of Voorstod, the Sweet Singer of Scaery, had gathered up her children and fled that accursed land. Voorstod was a place where women were nothing but the property of their husbands or fathers, a place where a child could be shot down in crossfire and the gunner would merely be criticized for his bad aim. It was a place where men used whips on the enslaved Gharmish people, where fanatics who would stop at nothing followed the way of Ire, Oron, and Voorstod to impose their will on humankind.

With her son Sam and her daughter Sal, Maire went to the pastoral colony of Hobbs Land. Originally Hobbs Land had been inhabited by the Owlbrit people, who had gradually died off. They had left behind several ruined temples and one whole one, complete with a god—a god who died after Sal and Sam were grown. No one connected the death of the Owlbrit god with the changes that followed. The children of Hobbs Land began to do strange and wonderful things. They rebuilt a temple, from the mosaic floors to the vaulted arches. They even found a god for the temple. The scenery of Hobbs Land began to change, too. Waterfalls, forests, and canyons appeared where none had been before. But would the changes be enough? Could the beauty and goodness of Hobbs Land defeat the spread of Voorstod's evil ways?

—*Di Herald*
Mesa County Public Library, Grand Junction, CO

Redwork

Michael Bedard. Macmillan, 1990. 272p. Hardbound (ISBN 0-689-31622-4) $15.95. **Grades 5–8. 3Q, 3P.**

When you don't have much money, you can't be choosy about where you live. Cass and his mother live in the second-floor apartment of a decrepit old house. Their landlord, Mr. Magnus, is so reclusive that Cass has never actually seen him. He and his mother just slip the rent check under his door every month.

Cass learns that Mr. Magnus is a World War I veteran, well over 90 years old, with a wooden leg and lungs damaged by poison gas. He never leaves the house except to go to the garage out back, where wisps of smoke can be seen coming from the chimney all night long. The neighbors say he's a witch and the neighborhood children are all terrified of him and won't go near the house.

Cass isn't surprised to hear that Mr. Magnus might be a witch. After all, he has shared some of the old man's nightmares about the war, and he found a mysterious drawing of the snake Ouroboros, the snake with its tail in its mouth that devours itself and is eternally reborn. But Cass is interested in more than nightmares—he wants to know the truth, and begins to investigate. Mr. Magnus, he discovers, isn't a witch, but an alchemist, searching for the philosopher's stone and all the secrets of life that go with it.

—*Rene Mandel*
Framington, MA

Scavenger Hunt

Christopher Pike. Pocket Books, 1989. 210p. Paperbound (ISBN 0-671-67656-3) $2.95. **Grades 7–12. 2Q, 3P.**

[Note: Photocopy or retype the list from pages 46–47 and distribute to the class before the booktalk begins.]

Mr. Partridge handed out the rules of the scavenger hunt to the members of the senior class after the teams had been formed. They would be competing for an all-expense-paid trip to Hawaii. Everyone thought it would be a lot of fun. Everyone was wrong.

What's your worst nightmare? Can you remember the worst nightmare you ever had, or what that nightmare might be? Maybe falling, maybe being chased, maybe something much worse. Take a second and think about that nightmare. [Pause.]

That nightmare is a good night's sleep compared to the nightmares that Carl has been having. In his nightmare, Carl and his best friend Joe are riding their bikes. They ride until they reach a dam. They stop for a moment and then ride on. On the other side of the dam, the weather changes.

Thunder cracks and lightning shoots from the sky, but not above them, only behind the dam. Suddenly there is a loud crash and something falls from the sky into the lake behind the dam. They start riding for home, but their tires get stuck in the mud. There's more thunder, more lightning, and the dam begins to break. But it isn't water that first oozes and then spurts out of the break in the dam—it's a thick red liquid that looks like blood. Then the dam bursts open and huge chunks of concrete fly through the air. Behind them is the thing that fell from the sky, a huge monster with red-hot eyes, riding a bloody wave right for Carl and Joe.

At first, Carl tries to forget the dream, only to discover that he can't—it haunts him. After the scavenger hunt begins, the nightmares get worse and worse. And when the hunt takes Carl into the desert, he recognizes it from his dream even before he sees the dam. As they pass the dam, he hears the thunder and sees the lightning. Looking back over his shoulder, he sees something fall from the sky, and the dam about to break. What happens when a nightmare comes true?

Take a look at your list of things to find on the scavenger hunt. Simple things, easy to find. Look again, and you'll see something else. You'll see the same thing Carl and the rest of his friends do—you'll see your worst nightmare come to life as part of the *Scavenger Hunt.*

—*Patrick Jones*
Allen County Public Library, Fort Wayne, IN

📖 Scorpions

Walter Dean Myers. HarperCollins, 1990.
224p. Paperbound (ISBN 0-06-447066-0)
$3.95. HarperCollins, 1988. 160p. Hardbound
(ISBN 0-06-024364-3) $13.00. **Grades 5–8.**
4Q, 3P.

Jamal hates school. Not because of the teachers, but because of the students. One other student. Dwayne. Dwayne is the school bully, and he seems to get a special kick out of picking fights with Jamal.

Jamal hates it at home. Not because of his mother, but because of his brother Randy. His older brother, who's in jail for holding up a restaurant. Jamal's mother is working hard to get money for an appeal, but it probably won't do any good, because even though Mama won't face it, Jamal knows that Randy probably did it.

Jamal hates the streets. He hates being surrounded by all the crime and violence that cities—and gangs—seem to bring. Jamal hates the gangs, especially the Scorpions. He knows a lot about the Scorpions because his brother Randy used to be their leader.

The Scorpions hate that Randy is in jail. Some members of the gang are glad to be rid of Randy, but Crazy Mack was Randy's best friend and he wants Randy back. And if he can't have Randy, then he'll take the next best

thing. He'll take Jamal. He'll make Jamal the leader of the Scorpions.

Jamal hates the idea of being the leader of the Scorpions. He's in junior high and he wants nothing to do with gangs, with drugs, with crime, and nothing at all to do with Crazy Mack. But Mack pushes and pushes him. Randy puts the word out on the street that he wants Jamal to take over. Jamal doesn't know what to do.

Jamal hates Dwayne and doesn't know what to do about him, either. Almost every day, Dwayne picks a fight with Jamal. Jamal wishes that he could win sometimes, instead of just fighting back. Jamal wishes he could be more powerful.

Crazy Mack hates it when Jamal turns him down, and he's determined not to take no for an answer. So he tells Jamal he has no choice. When Jamal tries to tell him he's too young, he's too scared, Crazy Mack just laughs. Crazy Mack has the solution to being too young and too scared—he hands Jamal a gun.

Jamal hates the gun. He knows the kind of trouble he could get into just for having it. When he holds it in his hand, he wishes he'd never seen it. But then when he holds it in his other hand, he remembers how he wished he could be more powerful. The gun makes him feel very, very powerful.

Jamal waits for Dwayne. He picks the time and place for the fight. He gets there ahead of time and makes sure everything is ready. Dwayne lands the first punch and knocks Jamal down. Jamal reaches behind him and pulls out the gun.

"That ain't real."

"Come on," Jamal shouted. "I'll show you it's real."

"That ain't nothing but a cap pistol."

"Come on and find out."

"Jamal, just who do you think you are?"

Jamal pointed the pistol right at Dwayne's face. "Haven't you heard? I'm the new leader of the Scorpions."

—*Patrick Jones*
Allen County Public Library, Fort Wayne, IN

📖 Send No Blessings

Phyllis Reynolds Naylor. Atheneum, 1990.
231p. Hardbound (ISBN 0-689-31582-1)
$13.95. **Grades 9–12. 4Q, 3P.**

What do eight kids and two parents all cooped up in a double-wide trailer equal? To Beth Herndon, the answer is frustration.

Her mother needs her to take care of her younger brothers and sisters. She has to squeeze in time to study after an evening spent making artificial flowers, flowers that pay for necessities like her new winter coat. And the trailer is so crowded and messy and shabby that Beth is ashamed to have her best friend, the daughter of a dentist, see where she lives.

All that Beth wants is to get away from the family that loves her and smothers her and keeps her from a better life. She can see only two ways out: she can graduate from high school and find a good job—but only if her father doesn't make her drop out and become a waitress—or she can marry Harless Prather, eight years older than she is, and happy working as a delivery man, with no ambition to ever do anything else. She loves Harless, but would marrying him trap her all over again, this time as a wife and a mother instead of a daughter? Beth is determined to get out of the rural West Virginia mountains where she's grown up and see the world she's only read about in books. Why do her parents seem determined to hold her back by urging her to get married?

Beth's mother calls her children "blessings from God," but Beth doesn't want any more blessings, hers or her mother's. All she wants is out.

—*Suzanne Bruney*
Lancaster, OH

Shadows in Bronze

Lindsey Davis. Crown, 1990. 341p. Hardbound (ISBN 0-517-57612-0) $19.00. **Grades 9–12, adults. 4Q, 4P.**

I'm going to give you some names, and I want you to tell me their occupations. James Bond [spy or secret agent]? Sherlock Holmes [private detective]? Miss Marple [investigator]? Thomas Magnum [private investigator]? Marcus Didius Falco [expect no answer, but someone may give an answer similar to the others, which is correct.]

Falco is one of the lesser-known spies and private investigators, perhaps because many of his investigations took place in Rome during the eighth century, A.D. 71, to be exact. But like many of his more modern counterparts, he's likable and witty, very vulnerable to wine and women, and above all, always solves the case.

Falco is working for the new caesar, Vespasian. Vespasian's road to the throne has been plagued with conspiracies and attempts at treason. Strange things begin to happen after a coup is dissolved and the key player, Atius Pertinax, son-in-law to a senator, is eliminated. An ex-slave of Pertinax's, now a freedman, is the prime suspect of a murder in one of the temples, and has begun following Falco. The new emperor wants Falco to notify the victim's brother of the murder, and discover why the ex-slave, Barnabas, is committing the crimes. Is he seeking revenge for his master's death, continuing the revolt, or just eliminating other conspirators?

Falco's investigations take him to the farms and villages around Moun Vesuvius. When he enters Pompeii, he cries in delight, "A place that intends to last!" (The eruption will not be for eight more years.) His entourage includes his close friend Petro, his wife Silva, their three daughters, an ox named Nero (and sometimes called Spot), and Falco's nephew Larius, who was sent along by his mother so Falco could serve as a good influence. They are sometimes accompanied by the love of Falco's life, the beautiful and outspoken Helena, widow of the traitor Pertinax.

As the mystery unwinds, there are enough adventures for everyone, and perhaps a few more than Falco would have preferred, including a battle at sea, a near-drowning (Falco can't swim), lavish parties, a mysterious wedding, love on a mountaintop, a rescue of Rome's grain ships, Nero's misguided attempts at passion with a donkey that land Falco and Larius in jail, and numerous attempts on everyone's lives.

Discover a few things you might not have known about eighth-century Italy, or about detectives.

—*Susan M. Weaver*
Kent State University, East Liverpool, OH

Slumber Party

Christopher Pike. Scholastic, 1985. 170p. Paperbound (ISBN 0-590-40927-1) $2.50. **Grades 7–12. 4Q, 4P.**

The road to the cabin was blocked with snow. Lara, Dana, and Celeste had to walk the last few miles to the cabin. Rachel, Nell, and Mindy had arrived several hours earlier. The six girls would be spending the weekend together. It was when they stood on the bluff above the cabin that Celeste began to ask questions and Lara and Dana decided to tell her the truth about Nell.

"We never told you about Nell. She was one of the gang when we were small. When we were nine years old, Nell had an accident. She got burned, and in a way, all of us were to blame. So we don't talk about it. I guess you would call it our deep, dark secret."

Now it was eight years later. Eight years after the accident, after the fire, after the screams, after the pain. Eight years later and five of the six girls from that party when Nell was injured are together again. Eight years of trying to forget for four of them. Eight years of plotting revenge for the fifth.

Why did the snowman near the house melt so quickly, suggesting that somehow someone had set it on fire? Why did someone take their car? Why did Dana vanish, leaving nothing behind but one ski and ashes? What did the message on the Ouija board mean? And why was there another fire?

It was eight years later. They all wanted to forget, but someone wanted them to remember, someone wanted them to pay. Do you want to hear a deep, dark secret? Go to the *Slumber Party*, if you dare.

—*Patrick Jones*
Allen County Public Library, Fort Wayne, IN

Someone Is Hiding on Alcatraz Island

Eve Bunting. Berkley, 1986. 144p. Paperbound (ISBN 0-425-10294-7) $2.99. Houghton Mifflin, 1984. 144p. Hardbound (ISBN 0-89919-219-X) $13.45. **Grades 5–8. 3Q, 3P.**

Who can tell me where Alcatraz Island is? Right, in California, in San Francisco Bay. Why is it famous? Right, it used to be a federal penitentiary, from which no one ever escaped. Now it's a national park and lots of tourists go there. So why am I asking about Alcatraz? Well, I'm asking because *Someone Is Hiding on Alcatraz Island.*

Danny is a good kid who wants to avoid trouble at school. Mostly he wants to avoid the school's roughest gang, the Outlaws. The most dangerous members of the Outlaws are Maxie, Jelly Bean, Cowboy, and Priest. Now you may be thinking that with names like those, they aren't so tough—but you're wrong, dead wrong. For instance, this kid named Jerry accidentally kicked Priest in gym class. He didn't do it again. Know why? It's kind of hard to kick someone after they've driven an ice pick through your foot. That's what Priest carries; no guns, no knife, just an ice pick. A very sharp ice pick.

But staying out of the Outlaws' way isn't easy, and Danny ends up where he doesn't want to be—running just as fast as he can, and only a few blocks ahead of a group of very angry Outlaws. They chase him down to Fisherman's Wharf. Danny ducks onto the ferry that goes to Alcatraz, not realizing that the Outlaws saw him and got on the next boat. Danny sees them as soon as it lands, and when Priest gets off, Danny knows he has his ice pick with him.

Thinking fast, Danny runs and hides inside the old prison. He's hiding in a cell when he overhears the Outlaws talking. They're standing right above him on the next tier of cells, talking and laughing about all the things they're going to do to Danny when they catch him—especially what Priest is going to do with his ice pick.

Danny waits and waits. Eventually he hears an announcement, "Last boat now leaving from Alcatraz Island." Still he waits and waits, all the time thinking how scared he is, and how he got himself into this mess. All the time thinking about the Outlaws, about Priest, about the ice pick.

Finally, a long time after the last boat left, Danny leaves the prison. He's all alone on an island in the middle of San Francisco Bay, he's cold, and he's afraid. But wait! This island is a national park, and all national parks have park rangers. He says to himself, "I'll go find the park rangers and I'll be safe." So he starts walking in the direction of the ranger station. He's about halfway there

when he sees a group of people walking toward him. "Rangers on patrol," he thinks, "now I'll finally be safe." So he starts walking toward them and they walk toward him and—wait a minute, park rangers don't carry . . . ice picks . . . .

—*Patrick Jones*
Allen County Public Library, Fort Wayne, IN

Squeaky Wheel

Robert Kimmel Smith. Dell, 1992. 182p. Paperbound (ISBN 0-440-40631-5) $3.50. Delacorte, 1990. 182p. Hardbound (ISBN 0-385-30155-3) $13.95. **Grades 3–6. 3Q, 2P.**

Mark started his first day of sixth grade scared and mad. Scared because he was late—his mother had overslept. Mad because he didn't want to be in this stupid new school, anyway. He wanted to be back in his old house, going to his old school with friends instead of strangers.

The kids in this new school had their own friends, and Mark felt left out. He missed his dad. Why did his parents have to get a divorce? They didn't even think about his feelings about moving away from the home he'd always known, or about hardly ever seeing his dad any more.

Should Mark tell his dad about wanting to spend more time with him? Should Mark tell his dad that he doesn't want to share him with his dad's new girlfriend and her daughter? Should he tell his mom how much he misses his old friends and his old school? Don't kids have any rights at all?

Mark's dad always told him, "The squeaky wheel gets the grease." What will happen if Mark decides to be that squeaky wheel?

—*Judy McElwain*
Mountain Home, WY

Taking Terri Mueller

Norma Fox Mazer. Avon, 1984. 192p. Paperbound (ISBN 0-380-79004-1) $3.50. Morrow, 1983. 224p. Hardbound (ISBN 0-688-01732-0) $12.95. **Grades 7–12. 3Q, 2P.**

How many of you have lived here in [insert name of city] all of your lives? How many have lived in this state? If Terri Mueller was in this class, she wouldn't have been able to raise her hand after either of those questions. You see, Terri Mueller, the girl you'll meet in this book, has lived in 15 different places. She doesn't really have any friends, because as soon as she gets to know someone, she and her father have to pack up and move again. Her father's her only friend and, except for her aunt, Terri's only family. When Terri was old enough to realize how different she was from everyone else, she asked her father about it. He told her that her mother had been killed in an auto accident when Terri was very young, and he'd rather not talk about it. So Terri doesn't have anyone to talk to, just more towns to come and go from every year.

Late one night while her aunt is visiting them, Terri overhears a conversation between her father and her aunt. What she hears Aunt Viv say makes her blood run cold: "When are you going to tell Terri the truth?" It's all she can think about at school the next day: "When are you going to tell Terri the truth?" It's all she can think about when she goes to sleep at night and when she wakes up in the morning. Finally, she tells her father that she overheard the conversation and wants to know what it meant. He refuses to tell her. But Terri knows she has to know the truth, whatever it is. She *has* to know.

A few days later, after school, Terri goes to her father's room and finds the box. It's a metal box with a lock on it, and it holds all their important documents—and Terri is sure it also holds the truth. "When are you going to tell Terri the truth?" keeps running through her mind as she breaks the lock with her jackknife and shuffles through papers and photographs. There are a lot of pictures of her father with a woman she doesn't know, and of a person who looks like her Aunt Viv, only much younger. Then she pulls out an official-looking document, thinking it's her mother's death certificate. It's not. It's a divorce certificate, dated a year after her father said her mother was killed. How could her parents get a divorce when her mother had been dead for a year? Can a ghost get divorced? Her father had lied. It was the only answer—but what was the truth? When would she know the truth about her mother, about her father, about herself?

Terri Mueller, the truth is that your mother is alive. You have lots of other relatives. When you were a baby, your father kidnapped you. And the reason you have to move all the time is that your mother has never stopped looking for you.

"When are you going to tell Terri the truth?" Now that you know the truth, Terri Mueller, what are you going to do about it?

—Patrick Jones
Allen County Public Library, Fort Wayne, IN

📖 That Was Then, This Is Now

S. E. Hinton. Dell, 1989. 224p. Paperbound (ISBN 0-440-98652-4) $3.50. Viking, 1971. 224p. Hardbound (ISBN 0-670-69798-2) $13.95. **Grades 7–12. 4Q, 3P.**

Mark and Bryon are best friends and they hang out together all the time. They do the same kinds of things you do with your friends, but mostly they get into trouble with teachers, parents, and other adults. Maybe they have too much time on their hands, but it isn't like

Mark doesn't have a hobby—if you can call hotwiring cars a hobby. Mark doesn't steal them, just borrows them for a while, rides around, and takes them back. And sure enough, one day his luck runs out. The police catch him, but his sentence is for probation.

When the time comes for him to report to his probation officer, Mark decides to blow it off. Bryon convinces him to go, but by that time he's already late and it's too far to walk, so he hotwires another car. But not just any car—the principal's car! Now, who's the principal here? Okay [point to person in audience], suppose it's lunch time, and you don't want to go in for the usual "death of the day," so you and some friends decide to go out for lunch. You hotwire [insert principal's name] car and go out. You come back with the windows down and the radio blaring, and when you pull up, [insert name] is there waiting for you. You know you're in big trouble. That's what happens to Mark, and you know what happens to him? Nothing. Why? Because Mark is one of those people—and you all know someone like this—who can talk his way out of anything. I mean, Mark could have a knife in his hand and a dead body with 20 stab wounds at his feet, and still convince you it was just an accident. In other words, he is a very smooth talker.

Mark uses this skill when he practices his other hobby: hustling pool. Mark and Bryon hang out in the local pool hall and win money from people. It isn't hard; they just act real young and goofy, and pretend they only play for fun. They act like they can't play very well when they're practicing, and when someone plays with them, they always let him suggest playing for money. Then they lose. They lose a lot, until it looks like the person playing with them is about to lose interest in beating them any longer. Then they suggest double or nothing. And that's when they show how they can really play.

On this particular day, after they hustle a couple of Texans, they start walking home. This is Bryon's story of what happened then:

"We're walking away and then we hear this voice, this Texas voice, say, 'Step right in the alley kiddies.' I froze because it was the voice of one of the Texans. So we walked down the alley. When we got to the end, we turned and faced the Texans. One guy was holding a gun on us while the other one was putting on a pair of brass knuckles. I could just imagine what my face was going to look like when he got through with me. I yelled at Mark to go, but he just said 'Guns, brass knuckles, or whatever, you know you've been in a fight if you tangle with me.' The Texan just laughed and spit. I backed up against the alley wall. There was no place to run. I was afraid that if I grabbed something to fight with or if I took a swing, the guy with the gun would shoot me. The Texan pushed me against the wall. He grabbed me with one hand, and with the other hand, the hand with the brass knuckles, he . . . ."

—*Patrick Jones*
Allen County Public Library, Fort Wayne, IN

A Time of Darkness

Sherryl Jordan. Scholastic, 1991. 241p. Paperbound (ISBN 0-590-43362-8) $3.25. Scholastic, 1990. 224p. Hardbound (ISBN 0-590-43363-6) $13.95. **Grades 7–12. 3Q, 3P.**

The firelight flickered on Rocco's sleeping face. The cave was warm and golden, the furs he slept in soft and comforting. But then a blackness passed by the mouth of the cave and yellow eyes gleamed in the firelight. As slight as the sound of the wolf gliding by was, it woke Rocco. He threw aside the furs and rolled to his knees. He was naked. Grabbing a blanket, Rocco pulled it around himself and stumbled to the firepit. A rich stew simmered above the flames. Rocco reached for a pottery bowl and ladled out some of the stew with a spoon carved from bone. Crouching on the floor, he began to eat, but paused, listening tensely to sounds outside the cave. Soundlessly putting the bowl and spoon on the earthen floor, Rocco stood, panting slightly like an animal, wary and afraid.

"Ayoshe?" he called out. He walked to the mouth of the cave and looked out. Only then did he remember that he should have brought a spear or at least a stick with him. He turned back. Then he saw it. The wolf was thin and mangy, its yellow eyes fixed on Rocco's face. It stalked past him into the cave as if it belonged there. Then it turned back towards Rocco, and he backed away onto the ledge outside the cave. The wolf pressed on and Rocco found himself on the very edge of the cliff, looking down to the rocks below. The wolf sprang at him, and Rocco felt himself falling, screaming.

He woke up, shaking and staring at the image of a wolf's head fading from sight on his bedroom wall. He still smelled smoke and stew and he ached all over. Rocco touched his cheek carefully. He remembered the wolf's teeth scraping the skin raw, yet now it felt normal, but sore.

The dream had returned, more vivid than ever. But was it only that? A dream? Rocco still smelled the smoke; he still felt as if he had been in the worst fight of his life. Yet his father, when he came into the room, smelled nothing and saw nothing wrong with Rocco's cheek.

Rocco didn't know what to think. Maybe he was going crazy. But it was so real. Was it time travel? Did his spirit visit the ancient past? Was it a premonition? Was it going to happen? Had it already happened? Rocco didn't know it, but the future of the entire human race depended on his finding the answers.

—*Julie Bray*
Jasper County Public Library, Rensselaer, IN

Tuck Triumphant

Theodore Taylor. Avon, 1992. 150p. Paperbound (ISBN 0-380-71323-3) $3.50. Doubleday, 1990. 150p. Hardbound (ISBN 0-385-41480-3) $14.95. **Grades 5–6. 3Q, 2P.**

The tiny six-year-old orphaned Korean boy arrived at the airport in Los Angeles with all his worldly possessions clutched in two small hands—a small straw bag and a tiny, dirty-gray, stuffed koala bear. The entire Ogden family was ready for the new adventure of learning Korean and teaching Chok-Do to speak English, until they learned he was both deaf and dumb. How could they possibly communicate with him?

Fourteen-year-old Helen Ogden knew she would find a way. After all, she was the one who taught her blind dog, a golden lab named Friar Tuck, to follow his own seeing-eye dog, a retired guide dog named Lady Rover. When Tuck went totally blind, some people had said that he should be put to sleep—it was the kindest thing to do. But Helen hadn't given up on Tuck, and she'd been right. He'd saved her life twice since becoming blind. And she wouldn't give up on Chok-Do, either. Together, she and Tuck and Daisy would find a way to reach him.

—*Marianne Tait Pridemore*
San Jose Public Library, San Jose, CA

Whalesinger

Welwyn Wilton Katz. Margaret K. McElderry Books, 1990. 212p. Hardbound (ISBN 0-689-50511-6) $13.95. **Grades 7–12. 3Q, 3P.**

"Breathe, calfling. Air is life. Breathe." She had heard a whale speak. The whale had called her calfling. It had spoken to her, Marty Griffiths, who could barely pass biology. A whale had spoken to *her*! The record of whale sounds Marty had heard in school hadn't been remotely close to the words, English words, she had heard the whale say. She had been watching the whale the whole time and its mouth hadn't moved, but a moment later the calf had joined its mother on the surface. If the mother had called it in her mind to come to the surface, could Marty somehow have tuned in to that communication and thought the whale was speaking to her? But how had she understood the whale? The more she thought about it, the more certain she became that she had imagined the conversation. Sick with disappointment, Marty sat quietly replaying the scene in her mind when she overheard another message from the whale. It had a half-amused tone to it, as if the whale were saying, "I'm not something you need to hold your breath about! Breathe, silly child, breathe!"

But discovering she could hear what the whale was thinking was only one of the adventures that Marty and her friend Nick had while on that field trip. They also learned that the trip was really a cover for an illegal search for sunken treasure. And that's when crooked scientists and nature gone crazy started to cause real problems for Marty, Nick, and the whales.

—*Anne Cowley*
Chambersburg Area Senior High School, Chambersburg, PA

Young Merlin

Robert D. San Souci. Illustrated by Daniel Horne. Doubleday, 1990. unp. Hardbound (ISBN 0-385-24800-8) $13.95. **Grades 3–8. 4Q, 3P.**

Camelot. King Arthur. The Knights of the Round Table. And Merlin the Magician. We've all heard of them. But where did they come from? How did it all start? It really started with Merlin. Without the great magician, Arthur and Camelot would never have existed. But where did Merlin come from?

Long ago in Wales, a stranger appeared in the village of Carmarthan. He had green eyes flecked with gold and always held a gold coin in his hand. He married the prettiest young woman in the village, and soon she was to have a child. When she told her husband, he seemed neither pleased nor displeased, but not long after, he disappeared without a word. The people of the village whispered that he must have been an elf or demon. The woman was blessed with holy water and went to live at a convent. There she gave birth to a son. He was named Merlin and he laughed, but never cried.

Merlin could see the unseen, read the future, and watch the past. He never used these gifts for wickedness, but nevertheless they could bring him sorrow, as they did when he foresaw his own mother's death. As he grew, so did his powers. He befriended the animals of the forest and rode a huge stag through the glens.

But the kingdom of England was not at peace. The war between King Vortigern and the rightful king of England soon came to the village of Carmarthan and to Merlin. His life was changed forever in the midst of a children's ball game. As a bully was taunting Merlin about his unhuman father, a knight of King Vortigern overheard and swept Merlin away to the king. Vortigern's wise men had told him that only the blood of a boy who had no human father would save the king's last and greatest fortress. The great castle had crashed to the ground three times for no reason, and the king believed that only Merlin's blood would make it stand firm. Merlin had only his second sight and his wits to save him from certain death.

To discover how Merlin saved himself, what he saw under the fortress, and how the great stone circle of Stonehenge was created, read *Young Merlin*.

—*Julie Bray*
Jasper County Public Library, Rensselaer, IN

A Knack for Knicknacks

By Bette D. Ammon, Missoula Public Library
and Gale W. Sherman, Pocatello Public Library, Pocatello, ID

Okay, you're sold on booktalking or you wouldn't be reading this. But (like the rest of us) you are always looking for more information and innovative ideas to inspire yourself and your listeners. So, the following is a variation on a booktalking theme: using props.

The best booktalking prop is the book itself—after all, the excitement and the pleasure come from reading that very book. But sometimes (just sometimes) it's nice to add some extra punch to a booktalk and provide something a little different to enhance your talks. Keeping in mind that the *book* is still the focus, a prop can attract attention and draw your audience in before they realize it. The key is simplicity: Don't allow the prop to distract from your talk or the book. The prop should be easy to handle and logically apply to the book you are talking about. Basically, a prop is simply a visual aid that arouses curiosity. "Why on earth does she/he have that?"

Using props can reap benefits in other ways, too. If you are encouraging and teaching students to do booktalks, instead of those deadly book reports, challenge them to include a prop. Of course, you will have to provide excellent examples for modeling!

Examples? Consider the following:

Letter Props

Return of the Indian. Lynne Reid Banks. Doubleday, 1986. 192p. ISBN 0-385-23498-X. $12.95.
[Prop: the letter printed on page 17, inside an envelope with Omri's name on the outside.]

When Omri gets home from school, his mother confesses she has accidentally opened a letter addressed to him. She is unable to contain her excitement and urges him to read it immediately. (Open envelope and read the entire letter:) "Dear Omri, We are delighted to inform you . . . ." Omri wants to share this news with Little Bear, the real plastic Indian. However, when he turns the key and opens the little cupboard where Little Bear lives, he discovers that Little Bear's life in the past year has been filled with turmoil and danger. Can Omri help Little Bear? Can the Indian return?

Cracker Jackson. Betsy Byars. Penguin, 1986. 146p. ISBN 0-670-80546-7. $12.95.
[Prop: a pink envelope with the unsigned letter printed on page 4.]

Things started to go wrong for Jackson on the day he received this anonymous letter. (Open letter and read:) "Keep away, Cracker, or he'll hurt you." Jackson looked at the letter and felt shaky all over. He wondered if anonymous letters are actually heavier than regular letters, because this letter was heavy enough to make him tremble. Do you wonder who wrote that letter . . . and why?

Sarah, Plain and Tall. Patricia MacLachlan. Harper-Collins, 1985. 58p. ISBN 0-06-024101-2. $10.95.
[Prop: a letter in an envelope with a cat drawn on the outside; content of letter printed on page 13.]

If you had to get a mother through the mail, what would you write to her? Would you ask her if she could keep a fire going all night . . . or if she snored? Caleb writes all those questions to Sarah. And she answers him. (Open prop letter and read entire letter:) "Dear Caleb . . . ." Sarah decides to visit Caleb, his sister Anna, and their Papa, but she may be too homesick for the sea to stay and be their mother.

The Sacred Moon Tree. Laura Shore. Bradbury, 1986. 224p. ISBN 0-02-782790-9. $13.95.
[Prop: letter printed on page 75.]

Twelve-year-old Phoebe becomes Feebus after she disguises herself as a boy in order to rescue her friend Jotham's brother, Nate, from a Rebel prison. The letter she leaves for her grandfather explains everything. (Read entire letter:) "Dearest Grandfather, Please do not be alarmed by our absence . . . ." Feisty Phoebe has always wanted to be involved in the action of the Civil War—and now she has a chance.

Notes as Props

The Blossoms and the Green Phantom. Betsy Byars. Delacorte, 1987. 160p. ISBN 0-385-29533-2. $13.95.
[Prop: a piece of paper with a list of materials written on it, as printed on pages 2–3 . . . "Garbage bags, String, Wire, Tape, Air mattresses, Patches for the air mattress, Day-Glo paint [green]." Be sure to turn down one corner of the paper. Begin this booktalk by reading the list of materials.]

Junior Blossom has collected all the materials on this list except the secret ingredient. That's written under this folded down corner. And he has to have that ingredient to complete the elaborate balloon he hopes will be identified as a UFO. What's the secret ingredient? Junior says it is "very, very, very important." Why on earth is Junior making a UFO anyway? Does it have anything to do with the aluminum cans Junior's grandfather is collecting when he gets trapped in a dumpster? And what does the Green Phantom have to do with it, anyway?

Space Demons. Gillian Rubinstein. Dial, 1988. 198p. ISBN 0-68037-0534-4. $13.95.

[Prop: a piece of paper with the following words in black marker: "DO NOT TURN OFF! VITAL! GAME IN PROGRESS!"]

Ben and Andrew are playing a strange computer game called "Space Demons." It's like a lot of other computer games, with lots of action and interaction. But something goes dreadfully wrong with this version—Ben is actually sucked into the game and disappears into the computer. A stunned Andrew remains behind, dreadfully confused about what to do next. And he's terrified about what might happen if somebody turned off the computer. Would Ben be lost forever? While he tries to figure this out, Andrew makes a sign to attach to his computer. (Hold up prop so audience can read it:) This sign may mean the difference between life and death.

The War with Grandpa. Robert Kimmel Smith. Delacorte, 1984. 128p. ISBN 0-385-29312-7. $12.95.

[Prop: a note typed as it appears on page 47.]

Ten-year-old Peter Stokes is thrilled that his grandfather is coming to live with his family, until he learns that Grandpa will be staying in Peter's own room. So Peter declares war. Now everyone knows that when you start a war, you have to let the enemy know about it. Peter lets Grandpa know that they are at war by leaving this note on his bed. [Read prop note:]

DECLARATION OF WAR!!!

YOU HAVE STOLEN SOMETHING THAT BELONGS TO ME . . .

The War with Grandpa has officially begun. But how will it end?

Signs

⚠ **Sudden Silence.** Eve Bunting. Harcourt Brace Jovanovich, 1988. 107p. ISBN 0-15-282058-2. $13.95.

[Prop: create a poster just like the one made by Jesse and Chloe, pictured on page 39 of the hardback edition.]

"DID YOU SEE WHAT HAPPENED ON COAST HIGHWAY

AT APPROXIMATELY 11:30 PM ON JUNE 20?

A SIXTEEN-YEAR-OLD BOY WAS HIT AND KILLED

BY A CAR THAT DIDN'T STOP."]

After his deaf brother, Bryan, is killed in a hit-and-run accident, Jesse becomes obsessed with finding the driver. Frustrated because he can't remember any details about the accident, Jesse agrees to work with Bryan's friend Chloe to put up posters to help gather information. (Hold up and read prop poster.) Clues lead Jesse to suspects in the neighborhood, but when he discovers the driver's identity, he also discovers that he now has a whole new set of problems.

Strider. Beverly Cleary. Morrow, 1991. ISBN 0-688-09900-9. $12.95.

[Prop: one piece of paper with the word "Sit" written on it, and one piece of paper with the word "Stay" written on it.]

When Leigh Botts finds an abandoned dog, he adopts it and names it Strider. Everything about Strider is wonderful. He loves to run with Leigh and responds well to nearly every command—except "Stay" and "Sit." When he hears those words, Strider trembles and looks frightened. Apparently his former owner used those commands on Strider, but then went away, never to return. However, Leigh is convinced that Strider is smarter than the average dog, so he teaches him to read. (Hold up prop signs.) Now when Strider sees this sign he . . . sits. And when he reads this sign he . . . stays. And Leigh never has to say a word.

Doctor de Soto. William Steig. Farrar, Straus & Giroux, 1982. 32p. ISBN 0-374-31803-4. $13.95.

[Prop: a sign designed like Dr. de Soto's shingle, shown on page 5 of the book.]

Doctor de Soto does dental work on most animals. However, because he is a mouse, he refuses to treat animals dangerous to mice. It says so on his sign. (Hold up prop and read: "Dr. de Soto, Dentist. Cats & Other Dangerous Animals Not Accepted For Treatment.") He and his wife looked out the window every time the doorbell rang and they absolutely would not let in even the nicest looking cat. But when a wily and persuasive fox comes by with a toothache, the kindly doctor just might be persuaded to change his mind.

Food Props

Beetles, Lightly Toasted. Phyllis Reynolds Naylor. Atheneum, 1987. 144p. ISBN 0-689-31355-1. $11.95.

[Prop: provide a brownie snack *before* doing this booktalk. Don't forget to add finely chopped nuts or rice cereal to the brownies to give the illusion of crunchy insects!]

Andy is conducting a science experiment on alternative protein sources. So he bakes his first batch of brownies, with beetles added, to share with his unsuspecting classmates. He wanted to see how they would react. You see, the beetles, scientifically speaking, really are good for you . . . they do provide additional protein. All Andy really wants to do is win a contest and have his picture featured in the local newspaper, just like every other member of his family. But the important thing is . . . will people like the taste of these brownies? And will they speak to Andy afterwards? What do you think?

Tape Recordings as Props

Losing Joe's Place. Gordon Korman. Scholastic, 1990. 192p. ISBN 0-590-42678-7. $12.95.

[Prop: enlist someone with a Joe-like voice to tape record the answering-machine message printed on page 18, beginning with "Hey, Jason . . . sorry I couldn't meet you guys . . . ."]

When Jason and his two summer roommates arrived at his brother Joe's apartment, the light on the answering machine was blinking. When they pushed the "listen" button, this is what they heard: (Play tape.) The title of this book says it all—*Losing Joe's Place*—so you can guess *what* happens, but you'll never guess *how*!

The Broccoli Tapes. Jan Slepian. Philomel Books, 1989. 157p. ISBN 0-399-21712-6. $13.95.

[Prop: a tape recording of the first paragraph of the book, "Testing. One, two, three, four. Testing. Is this tape recording working? . . . ," to be played at beginning of booktalk.]

This is how Sara begins her oral history project. She is recording what's happening in her life while she spends a semester in Hawaii. Living in a place everyone describes as Paradise is more difficult for Sara and her brother Sam than they thought it would be. But when they become involved in taming a wild cat that they name Broccoli, and making friends with an unhappy but interesting boy named Eddie, life in Hawaii becomes a lot more interesting and exciting.

Maps as Props

Danger in Quicksand Swamp. Bill Wallace. Holiday, 1989. 196p. ISBN 0-8234-0786-1. $14.95.

[Prop: a map similar to the one opposite the title page and colorfully described on page 44: "I could see lines in red and blue. They were faded and old-looking . . . ."]

Ben and Jake found this old map [hold up map prop] in a rowboat they dug out of a riverbed. After they looked at it a while, they realized it was a map of treasure buried in Quicksand Swamp. Now, Ben's Grandma told the boys they should always stay away from Quicksand Swamp. She said it was dangerous . . . and, it turned out, Grandma was right. If you like excitement, murder, kidnapping, alligators, quicksand, and danger, this is the book for you.

Other Props

The Wish Giver. Bill Brittain. Illustrated by Andrew Glass. HarperCollins, 1983. 181p. ISBN 0-06-020686-1. $12.70.

[Prop: wishing cards—a little white card with a red spot in the middle—for each listener.]

Imagine a carnival booth with a sign that says "Thaddeus Blinn. I CAN GIVE YOU WHATEVER YOU ASK FOR ONLY 50 CENTS." Would you take a look? The people who do discover that Mr. Blinn is selling wishes . . . yes, wishes! Mr. Blinn claims he deals in the incredible and promises that the wishes he sells will be very worthwhile. Would you buy one? (Pass out wish cards.) These are Mr. Blinn's wish cards. Have fun wishing. On second thought, wait. You might not be too anxious to spend your wish after you read *The Wish Giver* . . . you might just make a terrible mistake!

The possibilities are endless. Small toys can be used to grab attention while booktalking Lynne Reid Bank's *Indian in the Cupboard* (Doubleday, 1980) or Elizabeth Winthrop's *Castle in the Attic* (Holiday, 1985). A chess piece (the white pawn) is effective to use when booktalking Mary Shura's *The Josie Gambit* (Dodd, 1986). Some booktalkers hold a small, antique-looking bottle filled with magic water to intrigue readers with *Tuck Everlasting* by Natalie Babbitt (Farrar, 1975). One booktalker used a real football player as a prop when he booktalked *Quarterback Walk-on* by Thomas Dygaard (Morrow, 1982); another series of booktalks included a "corpse" on a table, appropriately draped with a sheet, while the booktalker gleefully talked about scary mystery stories. (Of course, the "corpse" appropriately waited to the end of the talk to sit up and scare everyone to death!)

The object of the activity (booktalking) is to capture potential readers' interest and imaginations and have a great time in the process. Using props with booktalks is just one more method we can use to successfully accomplish what we do the best—hooking kids on books!

Outstanding Titles
for the Reference Shelf

Genreflecting
A Guide to Reading Interests in Genre Fiction
3d Edition

Betty Rosenberg and Diana Tixier Herald

This best-selling guide to genre fiction has been expanded and updated to provide information on the newest popular fiction. It covers westerns, thrillers, science fiction, fantasy, supernatural/horror fiction, and romance. It defines the various genres; analyzes their characteristics; groups authors according to type or subject content; and provides a selective, annotated bibliography of the history and criticism of each genre.

**1991 xxv, 345p. ISBN 0-87287-930-5
$35.00**

American Indian Reference Books
for Children and Young Adults

Barbara J. Kuipers

All school and public libraries should own this title.–Preview

An annotated bibliography of more than 200 recommended reference books on American Indians for grades 3-12. Annotations are lengthy and discuss the strengths and weaknesses of each book and its potential use in the curriculum.

**1991 xiv, 176p. ISBN 0-87287-745-0
$25.00**

Wordless/Almost Wordless Picture Books
A Guide

Virginia H. Richey and Katharyn E. Puckett

This useful reference for librarians, preschool and elementary teachers, ESL teachers, and literacy program coordinators describes a wide selection of titles, including books in which the illustrations provide the complete story, alphabet and number books, concept books, and books with minimal text. Each entry contains a brief annotation and lists themes linked to the story. Also includes a comprehensive theme and subject index.

**1992 xvi, 223p. ISBN 0-87287-878-3
$27.50**

Literature Activity Books
An Index to Materials from Whole Language
and Shared Literature

Marybeth Green and Beverly Williams

Now you have easy access to ideas and activities for more than 1,000 quality children's books. This work provides an integrated author, title, and subject arrangement and lists teacher idea books that extend children's trade titles. Use it to find materials to support a particular title, author, or subject. An excellent planning tool.

**1993 viii, 203p. ISBN 1-56308-011-7
$27.00**

Crafts Index for Young People

Mary Anne Pilger

There is something for every possible craft need in this index! More than 20,000 craft activities are indexed in nearly 1,200 books. Things to make include costumes, masks, clay projects, ornaments, models, cards, sculptures, needlecrafts, tile, collages, carvings, and more. Entries are arranged by subject with extensive cross-referencing.

**1992 viii, 286p. ISBN 1-56308-002-8
$32.50**

Holidays and Special Days Project Index
for Young People

Mary Anne Pilger

More than 7,000 entries covering a variety of holidays (American holidays, holidays in other lands, special days like Stamp Day and Arbor Day, and festivals) lead to exciting projects–recipes, activities, puppets, decorations, crafts, games, and more–in nearly 1,200 books. Entries are arranged by subject and extensively cross-indexed.

**1992 viii, 160p. ISBN 0-87287-998-4
$29.50**

**To order call or write
Libraries Unlimited, Dept. 27:
1-800-237-6124
P.O. Box 6633, Englewood, CO 80155-6633**

Biographies and Fictionalized Biographies

An Actor's Life for Me

Lillian Gish. Nonfiction. Viking, 1987. 73p.
Hardbound (ISBN 0-670-80416-9) $14.95.
Grades 3–6. 4Q, 3P.

Lillian Gish was born about 95 years ago, and she made *The Whales of August* when she was 92! Because she started acting when she was just 6, she's been working as an actress for 86 years!

When Lillian started her career, there were no TVs, movies, or airplanes. There were a few cars, but most people used horses or trains to get around. Lillian, her sister Dorothy, and their mother rode the train to get from job to job. They were part of a group of traveling actors who stayed in each town just long enough to give one performance of their show, performing in a different town every night. For the people in those little towns, seeing a play was a big event, because they got to see only two or three plays a year.

Lillian enjoyed parts of her life—no school, dressing up and acting every night—and getting paid for it! But some things really weren't fun at all, like dirty hotel rooms, with none of the conveniences in them that we have today, and sleeping in cold, bumpy trains, knowing that she had to be rested for the performance the next day—no yawning on stage! And some of the parts Lillian had to play were difficult, or dangerous, or both. In one, Lillian was supposed to "fly" across the stage, but her support wire snapped and she fell. In another play, she was accidentally shot with buckshot while she was on stage—but she finished the play anyway. One of her least favorite memories is of the play where she was thrown into a lion's cage—with a live lion in it!

But Lillian loved the actor's life in spite of it all. As she got older, she got better at it, and when "flickers" were invented, Lillian became a movie star!

Would you love an actor's life the way Lillian did?

—*Julie Bray*
Jasper County Public Library, Rensselaer, IN

Anonymously Yours

Richard Peck. Nonfiction. Julian Messner,
1991. 122p. Hardcover (ISBN 0-671-7416-6)
$12.95. **Grades 5–12. 3Q, 2P.**

As an American student attending a British university for a year, Richard knew that he would be in for some new experiences, but this one scared the daylights out of him. He couldn't believe what he was hearing.

"Mr. Peck, I have an assignment for you," Professor Salter said. "The university is asking a group of foreign students to speak on a panel about the educational system in their countries. You will speak for the United States. A 10-minute presentation. Wednesday."

Did Professor Salter know Richard's frightening secret? Or did the professor think that, because this young American planned to be a teacher, speaking before a group of people wouldn't bother him? Well, it *did* bother him—a lot! To the point of dry-mouthed, tight-throated terror. And 10 minutes? It might just as well be 10 hours!

But there was no escaping the truth—to achieve his goal of becoming a teacher, Richard had to get over his fear of speaking before groups. Professor Salter provided his cure. That Wednesday, as he left the stage, Richard realized that he was cured. Little did he know then that he would talk not only to classrooms of teenagers, but also, as a well-known author, to audiences of hundreds of teachers and librarians all over the world.

You may have read Richard Peck's books, but you probably don't know how many memories and personal experiences are sprinkled through them: the gorilla suit from *Remembering the Good Times*, the former student who was the model for Pod in *Princess Ashley*, and Blossom Culp, whose origins are as complex as her character.

Have a look at the characters you've met and the situations you've seen—and perhaps some you haven't—from a different point of view, through the eyes of the man who created them, Richard Peck himself.

—*Nancy Chu*
Western Illinois University, Macomb, IL

The Big Lie

Isabella Leitner. Nonfiction. Scholastic, 1992.
80p. Hardcover (ISBN 0-590-45569-9)
$13.95. **Grades 3–6. 3Q, 3P.**

I grew up in the small town of Kisvarda, Hungary, in the 1940s. War was raging across Europe, but in our small town, things were quiet. Our little town was too insignificant to be important to Hitler's Nazi soldiers. But on March 20, 1944, all that changed. It is a day I will never forget, because that day, the war reached our town, and all of our lives changed forever.

The war did not come with bullets and bombs, but with edicts. Edicts that said all Jews were required to wear yellow stars on their clothing. Jewish children could no longer attend the public school. And those were only the first—every day they became more and more restrictive. Jews were not allowed to own radios or bicycles. Jews could not be outside after 7:00 p.m. Then one day the soldiers came and told us we could no longer live in our own house. All Jews had to live together in an old run-down ghetto.

May 28, 1944, was my birthday, but there was no reason to celebrate. That was the day we were told to be ready for deportation at 4:00 the next morning. We were headed, although we didn't know it at the time, to the Nazi death camp at Auschwitz.

—*Linda Olson*
Superior Public Library, Superior, WI

Bill Peet: An Autobiography

Bill Peet. Nonfiction. Houghton Mifflin, 1989. 190p. Hardbound (ISBN 0-395-50932-7) $16.95. **Grades 3–6. 4Q, 3P.**

[Bring two or three of Peet's books along and hold them up, asking if any of the kids have read them.]

Do any of you remember reading these books when you were younger? Bill Peet isn't just an author and illustrator, though. He used to work for Walt Disney. Have you seen *Cinderella*? Bill Peet did the mice in that movie. What about *Alice in Wonderland* or *Peter Pan*? Bill Peet worked on both of them. And have you seen *101 Dalmatians* or *The Sword in the Stone*? Bill Peet created both of them, from start to finish!

Of course, Bill didn't start off working on those big projects, or even working for Walt Disney. He started out in Indiana, and grew up in Indianapolis. He started drawing as soon as he could hold a pencil or a crayon, and he got in trouble in school because he drew too much of the time. He liked to draw animals, locomotives, and especially weird critters. [Show page 6.] One day Bill tried to catch a large frog so he could draw it—and this is what happened. [Show pages 11–14.]

As he got older, Bill's drawing got better, and he won some money with a few paintings. But then there was the Depression of the 1930s, when lots of people were out of work. There were too many people and not enough jobs, and Bill had to figure out how to make money. Work for Walt Disney, maybe? So Bill left Indiana for California and a career in the movies.

By the way, who's seen *The Little Mermaid*? Bill's son worked on that movie.

—*Julie Bray*
Jasper County Public Library, Rensselaer, IN

The Dragon in the Cliff

Sheila Cole. Illustrated by T. C. Farrow. Lothrop, 1991. 211p. Hardcover (ISBN 0-688-10196-8) $13.95. **Grades 7–12. 4Q, 3P.**

I was in my shop, working on a fossil the day after Henry de la Beche and I had gone curiosity hunting in the clay over at Golden Cap, when the bell on the door rang, and I looked up to see Mrs. Gleed enter the shop.

"I have come to talk to you about your disgraceful conduct, Mary," she said, getting right down to business. "You have been seen many times walking alone on the beach with young Mr. de la Beche. The whole town is talking about you."

"But I've done nothing wrong," I protested, trying to defend myself from this unwarranted attack.

"Your behavior is unseemly," she said, cutting me off. "You didn't listen to your mother, so now you'll have to listen to me."

"We haven't done anything wrong!" I exclaimed. "We were hunting for curiosities. He pays me for what I find."

"Humph! Is *that* what he pays you for?"

"You know it is!" I screamed, losing my temper. I'd disliked Mrs. Gleed since the day she'd talked to Mama about sending me to chapel school. Now I hated her. How dare she tell me what to do! Didn't she realize that I had to support Mama and Joseph, now that Papa was dead?

"He pays me to take him curiosity hunting," I said, glaring at her. "Am I to stop earning a living just because of some gossip? We did nothing wrong!"

"I can see there's no use talking to you, Mary. You are determined to be wicked and will not repent," she said, and with that she turned on her heel and left.

Then I knew I could never be accepted by our neighbors as long as I collected fossils. Mrs. Gleed's vicious tongue would see to that. But I can no more give up fossils than I can give up breathing. They are a part of me. Why can't other people just accept me the way I am?

In 1811, 13-year-old Mary Anning found the first complete ichthyosaur skeleton. In an era when women were supposed to stay home and take care of their families, she became one of the leading paleontologists of her time.

—*Kathy Ann Miller*
SLIM student, Emporia State University, Emporia, KS

Famous Asian Americans

Janet Nomura Morey. Illustrated by Wendy Dunn. Nonfiction. Cobblehill Books, 1992. 170p. Hardbound (ISBN 0-525-65080-6) $15.00. **Grades 5–12. 4Q, 2P.**

As Dustin watched in horror, his friend was shot and died instantly. Dustin had to continue to swim toward the boat alone. Leaving Vietnam was not only difficult and expensive, it was dangerous. But Dustin was determined to get to the United States. He did, and this is who he is today [show portrait of him]—a successful actor who plays a policeman on "21 Jump Street," and who works hard to help kids stay away from drugs and gangs.

Leaving the country where you've grown up and going to a different one isn't easy, especially when you don't know the language, the customs, or the people. Especially when you don't know what you can do to earn a living. Some of the Asian immigrants who have come to the United States have been able to do more than just survive and support themselves and their families. Some have become so successful that they have been able to make a real impact on their adopted country, and change or benefit it in many ways. Dustin campaigns against drugs, using his reputation as an actor. An Wang, a Chinese immigrant and Harvard graduate, founded a computer company and changed the way we use computers, desktop calculators, and word processing systems.

Asian immigrants have become doctors, lawyers, writers, professors, politicians, and actors. Meet some of them here and discover how they have enriched and changed the United States with their unique contributions.

—*May Harn Liu*
University of South Carolina, Columbia, SC

📖 Gentle Annie: The True Story of a Civil War Nurse

Mary Frances Shura. Nonfiction. Scholastic, 1991. 184p. Hardcover (ISBN 0-590-44367-4) $12.95. **Grades 5–12. 4Q, 4P.**

A fresh load of patients had just been brought onto the boat. A young man with a chest wound groaned as Annie began to peel the blood-hardened bandage from his chest. He twisted as she worked and gave a weak cry of pain. "I'll try not to hurt you," she said. When she released the clotted bandage, she was shocked to see that half his chest had been blown away, and she could see his slowly beating heart. She tried to conceal her anguish, but he saw it in her eyes. "How much time for me, Annie?" he asked. How could she answer him? She knew that even the most skilled surgeons could not save him. All she could do was hold his hand while he died. She had seen many soldiers die since this bloody war had begun, but this one was different. Annie knew him. He was her friend.

She remembered her excitement when, three days before her seventeenth birthday, she'd enlisted with the Second Michigan Volunteer Regiment. She'd told her friends that now, at last, she knew what she wanted to do

with her life. Now all she wanted to do was go home, but she knew she couldn't let her regiment down.

Annie B. Etheridge, Civil War nurse, risked her life over and over again, dodging bullets while she cared for the wounded on the battlefields.

—*Kathy Ann Miller*
SLIM student, Emporia State University, Emporia, KS

📖 Growing up Cowboy: Confessions of a Luna Kid

Ralph Reynolds. Nonfiction. Fulcrum, 1991. 180p. Paperbound (ISBN 1-55591-086-6) $12.95. **Grades 9–12, adults. 4Q, 2P.**

Imagine yourself waking up in an unheated log cabin in the canyon county of New Mexico. You're on vacation, perhaps? No, you're about to slip into the shoes of Ralph Reynolds, as he and his father have to weather an early winter blizzard to drive the cattle down off the mesa to safety.

In the spring, you'll be slapping dust off your jeans after a long day of calf branding in the corral. But you've learned a few tricks from old cowpokes Max and Lamar, so at least you haven't gotten kicked. Nudged pretty hard, but not kicked. And if an ornery old mule wanders off into the brush, you know that you, the Luna Kid, will get scratched up in the thickets trying to find it.

Living on a ranch in the west of 50 years ago wasn't easy, but it did have its compensations—the country was unspoiled and majestic, and there were friends and family to share the battle to survive. Each season brought its own work, dangers, rewards, and adventures. Adventures like climbing in those old cave dwellings up the cliff. You find a clay pot left there 500 years before and carry it home, never expecting to create the mess that results. Rewards like the stunning view from the top of a fire tower. Dangers like taking a load of melons to market . . . Wait a minute—taking melons to market is dangerous? If you happen to find a melon that's a tarantula family's favorite, it can be! They may decide to go along for the ride, making both picking melons and unloading them at the market yet another hazardous occupation for a kid *Growing up Cowboy*!

—*Mark Anderson*
Fairfax County Public Library, Fairfax, VA

📖 Kaffir Boy

Mark Mathabane. Nonfiction. NAL, 1987. 350p. Paperbound (ISBN 0-452-25943-6) $9.95. **Grades 9–12, adults. 4Q, 3P.**

Mark Mathabane grew up in the ghetto of Alexandra, 10 miles north of Johannesburg, South Africa. His bed was a piece of cardboard under the kitchen table, and from birth, he had to endure police raids on his neighborhood. Mark feared the police, both black and white, and for a good cause—when he was five, he was beaten for not telling the police where his parents were. He also feared his parents. In the desperate place where Mark grew up, most boys ended up in a gang or dead in the gutter from drugs. The only way his parents knew to prevent it was to put fear into him, so they beat him too. Mark grew to hate his father, but loved his mother in spite of the screaming and beatings. He could sense she still loved and feared for him.

When Mark started to school, his mother made sure he had a note pad and a uniform. The sacrifices she had to make to do that simple thing were unbelievable. Schools for blacks in South Africa bear little resemblance to even the worst schools in this country. There are no desks, no supplies, and almost no books. The books that are available are old, outdated, and tattered. Dozens of kids are crammed into a room with a teacher, who frequently doesn't know much more than the students. It is a very effective way for the white government to keep the black population from pulling themselves out of the pit of poverty and despair created for them by that same government. Most black children grow up to lives of despair and poverty, working for whites. But Mark saw school as a way out, a way up. He was determined to learn all that he could, and by sheer force of will, became a superior student. He also discovered tennis, which turned out to be a way to escape the environment he'd grown up in. He soon was good enough to win matches in the black leagues—but would the whites' system of apartheid let him go further than that? Could tennis be the ticket out that Mark had spent his whole life looking for? Could it be a ticket to America?

—*Julie Bray*
Jasper County Public Library, Rensselaer, IN

📖 Land Circle: Writings Collected from the Land

Linda Hasselstrom. Nonfiction. Fulcrum, 1991. 349p. Hardbound (ISBN 1-55591-082-3) $19.95. **Adults. 4Q, 3P.**
Reviewed in: PW, 10/4/91, p. 74; Utne, 1/92, p. 120; Bloomsbury Review, 7/8/92, p. 1.

Which midwestern state is so forgettable that it was left out of a major atlas? South Dakota—a land of bone-chilling winters and sweltering summers, where fires and droughts and snakes and bears threaten human life. South Dakota—where making a living on a farm or ranch means constant, grinding work. Why on earth would anyone *choose* to live there?

Linda Hasselstrom tells you why. Linda left the city to live on a cattle ranch near the Black Hills with her husband, and since his death has managed the ranch by herself. Her life isn't pretty—it's tough and bloody and dirty. Yet it has its rewards: she lives in harmony with land and animals and knows she can survive alone.

As Linda learns, the only way to survive alone in South Dakota is to understand the ways of the West. How do you help a cow give birth? How do you harvest buffalo berries? Which flower petals are edible? Which boots will keep your feet from freezing? Why are horses blown up with dynamite? Why leave tobacco in tree notches? Why breed cows to small-headed bulls? How do you fight a forest fire? How do you build a house? Linda shares country wisdom essential to survival with you.

But this isn't just a how-to book. It's also part diary, one sensitive woman's moving journal of love and grief, as she watches her husband die of cancer; of courage, as she buys a gun for self defense; of humor, as she compares how men and women relieve themselves in the wilderness.

This book is also part politics, a declaration on the environment and animal rights that makes Linda's priorities clear. Yes, she will fight to save the pure Dakota air, but yes, she will also eat the meat of the cow she butchers.

Finally, this book is part poetry, blending Indian legends, cowboy folklore, and personal reflections. Listen to these lines from her poem "White Buffalo":

A white buffalo stands
at the hall's end. His mane
brushes the ceiling; frost
glitters on his beard. He stomps
a black hoof, shakes his head.
Ice shards clatter
on marble but no one hears.

Take a trip into the land of the White Buffalo, into forgotten South Dakota. Explore one of the last frontiers, one that most people know nothing about. You may discover that, like Linda Hasselstrom, you will never want to leave the Land Circle.

—*Therese L. Broderick*
Albany Public Library, Albany, NY

📖 The Land I Lost

Huynh Quang. Illustrated by Vo-Dinh Mai. Nonfiction. HarperCollins, 1986. 128p. Paperbound (ISBN 0-06-440183-9) $3.50. HarperCollins, 1990. 128p. Hardbound (ISBN 0-397-32447-2) $12.95. **Grades 5–8. 3Q, 3P.**

What do you know about Vietnam? Do you know about the Vietnam War and the thousands of American soldiers who died on the battlefields there? Have you been told about the protests in the United States by those who believed we should not be involved in the war? What pictures come to mind when you think of Vietnam? What stories about the people who live there?

But what if I told you that Vietnam was peaceful, a beautiful land filled with farmers, families and children who loved and worked together? Come with me to the village where Huynh Quang Nhyong lives. Meet his family, with their water buffalo Tank, and the other villagers, and listen to the stories they have to tell of a Vietnam you won't see in your history books. Discover a people that may have been strangers, that could have been enemies, but now can be called friends, and share the adventures of a boy growing up in Vietnam.

—*Susan Trimby*
St. Martin of Tours School, Kankakee, IL

Living Dangerously

Doreen Rappaport. Nonfiction. HarperCollins, 1991. 117p. Hardbound (ISBN 0-06-25108-5) $13.95. **Grades 5–8. 4Q, 2P.**

Bravery comes in many forms. Here you will find six kinds of courage in stories of women who weren't afraid to challenge the world to achieve their goals.

What would you have done if you were penniless, 63 years old, and single in 1921? Annie Taylor had always amazed her family and friends with her unusual lifestyle. As a result, it wasn't too surprising to them that Annie decided to try for fame and fortune by going over Niagara Falls in a barrel. Annie was sure she could do it, in spite of the fact that most of the men who had tried it had been dashed to bits on the rocks at the bottom.

What about Annie Smith Peck? She'd become one of the first women college professors in the United States, but it wasn't enough to satisfy her. She had done the difficult, but she wanted to try the impossible. So she challenged a mountain in Peru that no one had ever been able to climb.

Fullfillment for Bessie Coleman meant that she became a pilot at a time when most people had never even seen an airplane. And Bessie not only became a pilot, she became a barnstormer, a special kind of stuntflying daredevil who pushed the small planes she flew to their mechanical limits.

Whether it was in the depths of the ocean, the remote reaches of the jungle, or the streets of Manhattan, these women pushed themselves to the edge in their search for adventure, because of their decisions to spend their lives *Living Dangerously*.

—*Sue Young*
Ysleta Independent School District, El Paso, TX

Lost on a Mountain in Maine: A Brave Boy's True Story of His Nine-Day Adventure Alone in the Mount Katahdin Wilderness

Donn Fendler, as told to Joseph B. Egan. Nonfiction. Beech Tree Books, 1992. 109p. Paperbound (ISBN 0-688-11573-X) $3.95. Picton Press, 1978. 125p. Hardbound (ISBN 0-912274-92-1) $14.95. **Grades 5–8. 2Q, 2P.**

In July 1939, Donn Fendler got tired of waiting for his guide to lead him back to camp, so he took off on his own into the mists of Mount Katahdin. Nine days later, his body bleeding from cuts and thousands of insect bites, he emerged from the forest over 50 miles away. This is his story of survival.

Donn never really believed that someone could get as lost as he was in the United States of America, or that so many days could go by without his seeing a soul. He kept expecting a camp around every bend of the river. There never was one.

During the first days, he lost both his shoes and his pants. With only minimal survival skills, every day was an agony of sharp rocks, thorns, encounters with bears, and the ever-present need for food. This book may read like something out of a Gary Paulsen novel, but this isn't a novel, it's a real-life survival story told by the man who lived through it.

—*Jeff Blair*
Olathe South High School, Olathe, KS

Magnetic North: A Trek across Canada from the Pacific to the Atlantic by Foot, Dogsled and Canoe

David Halsey and Diana Landau. Nonfiction. Sierra Club Books, 1990. 252p. Hardbound (ISBN 0-87156-746-6) $19.95. **Grades 9–12, adults. 3Q, 2P.**

Are there any frontiers left anymore? Are there any adventures that will test someone, force him to his physical, mental, and emotional limits, and then push him out the other side a man? That's what David Halsey wanted to know after a restless, dissatisfied year at college. One thing he did know: what he was looking for didn't come ready-made. He would have to make it happen. If he finished, he would become the first person to trek a wilderness route across Canada, from one ocean to the other, traveling only by foot, dogsled, or canoe.

Did he have what it would take? David himself couldn't answer that question as he shouldered his pack for the first leg of his journey. But the adventures, disasters, and terrors he found along the way threatened to end his journey and his life, and turned a typical suburban kid into an explorer worthy of the name. Like a magnet, the challenge of the North pulled him forward to find the answers to the questions he never thought he'd ask.

—Pamela Todd
John A. Logan College, Carterville, IL

📖 Martin Luther King: Free at Last

David A. Adler. Nonfiction. Holiday House, 1986. 46p. Paperbound (ISBN 0-8234-0619-9) $4.95. Holiday House, 1986. 46p. Hardbound (ISBN 0-8234-0618-0) $12.95. **Grades 3–6. 4Q, 3P.**

When Martin was a kid, he had two friends, brothers, that he played with almost every day. Mostly they played baseball, and it was fun. One day, Martin's friends weren't at the park, so he went to their house. His friends' mother told him that he couldn't ever play with them again. His friends were white and he was black. Martin ran home and cried.

Would you understand if someone told you that you couldn't play with a friend because you have blue eyes and your friend has brown eyes? Or because your hair is curly and your friend's is straight? Martin's mother tried to explain why some white people feel it's necessary to keep black people away from them, but it didn't make Martin feel any better. It didn't make any sense to him, and when he got older, he decided to do something about it. But even though the ways the whites acted was cruel and unfair, Martin decided to fight back peacefully. Change couldn't come from hatred—there was too much of that already. Change had to come through peace. If a white man pushed him, Martin would let him. If a white person spat on him and called him names, Martin would just keep going on. Martin Luther King, Jr., was a great man of peace, but there were forces of evil and hatred fighting against him, forces who wanted him dead.

—Julie Bray
Jasper County Public Library, Rensselaer, IN

📖 Memories of My Life in a Polish Village, 1930–1949

Toby Knobel Fluek. Illustrated by Toby Knobel Fluek. Nonfiction. Knopf, 1990. 110p. Hardbound (ISBN 0-394-58617-4) $19.95. **Grades 3–8, adults. 4Q, 4P.**

Does your family have a photograph album with pictures of you when you were little, or of your parents when they were younger? Pictures of relatives? Holiday celebrations? The place you used to live? Pictures are a way to preserve your past, your unwritten history. Toby Fluek preserved her past as a Jewish girl growing up in Poland during World War II and shares it with you in her picture album, *Memories of My Life in a Polish Village*.

But Toby's picture album is different from the ones you and I have. Toby's pictures are ones she drew herself, from memory, because she has no photographs of her childhood. Everything that Toby had when she was young was taken away when the Nazis invaded Poland. The Nazis hated the Jews and punished them because they had a different religion.

Toby remembers that hatred—the price of being Jewish. She remembers having to give up her nice home and all her belongings to move to a crowded, run-down shack inside a fenced area with all the other Jews. She remembers being hungry and having nothing to eat for days at a time. She remembers having to hide to stay alive. She remembers being separated from her family and not knowing if they were dead or alive. She remembers being alone. But most of all, she remembers being afraid. But Toby also remembers happy times: life before the Nazi terror, finding her mother after the war, falling in love and coming to America. Share Toby's life in her picture album, and discover what it was like to be a young Jew before, during, and after the Nazis invaded Poland.

—Sandra Carpenter
Hamilton Elementary School, Hamilton, KS

📖 The Moon and I

Betsy Byars. Nonfiction. Messner, 1992. 96p. Hardbound (ISBN 0-671-74166-7) $12.95. **Grades 5–8. 4Q, 4P.** Reviewed in: Bklst, 5/15/92, p. 1675.

[Display a group of Byars's books and talk about some of them before starting this talk.]

Have you ever wished you could be an adult so you could do all the things you can't do because you're too young? I'll bet you have—I know I have. But even after Betsy Byars was an adult, she still didn't have something she'd wanted since she was a little girl. In this book, *The Moon and I*, she tells you all about it.

When she was a little girl, she wanted to grow up as fast as she could, so she could have all the pets she wanted, including a snake! But it took her 40 years to get that snake, and it slithered into her life when she least expected it. Why did she name it Moon? How did they meet and get to know each other? It's all here, and more, because Moon wasn't her only snake, just her first. Sometimes childhood dreams do come true—and in the strangest ways!

—*Sister M. Anna Falbo, CSSF*
St. Aloysius Gonzaga Convent, Cheektowaga, NY

📖 One More River to Cross: Stories of Twelve Black Americans

Jim Haskins. Nonfiction. Scholastic, 1992.
160p. Paperbound (ISBN 0-590-42896-9)
$13.95. **Grades 5–8. 4Q, 3P.**

In this book you'll meet 12 Americans who could be described as determined, brave, courageous, and followers of their dreams. Several were orphaned at an early age, the majority of them were very poor, and most were either uneducated or had to work very hard for their education. All were discriminated against for one reason or another. They were, for the most part, unappreciated, unrecognized, and unrewarded—all because of the color of their skin.

The first American to die in the American Revolution was a runaway slave, Crispus Attucks, but it was over a hundred years before a monument was dedicated to him.

Who was the first American woman to earn over a million dollars? In the early 1900s, Madame C. J. Walker developed and sold hair care products for black women, and became a millionaire.

Matthew Henson was one of the first two men to reach the North Pole, but like Crispus Attucks, it was many years before he received the recognition and honor he had earned.

Charles R. Drew discovered blood plasma and how it could be stored until it was needed for emergency blood supplies. Yet he had to educate people that all blood is the same. Blood from black people didn't have to be kept separate from the blood of white people.

Do you know the "winningest" coach in football? Eddie Robinson from Grambling College in Louisiana, who was also the first coach to provide drinking water for his players on the field during games.

In 1986, when the space shuttle Challenger caught fire, killing all seven astronauts aboard, you may remember that one of the crew was teacher Christa McAuliffe. But did you know that another crew member was also planning to be a teacher? His name was Ron McNair, and he was black.

These 12 Americans dreamed, worked for their dreams, and saw them come true. Perhaps their examples will help you keep on working for your own dreams. They just could come true.

—*Dorothy Davidson*
Jackson Elementary, Abilene, TX

📖 Outward Dreams: Black Inventors and Their Inventions

Jim Haskins. Nonfiction. Bantam, 1991. 102p.
Paperbound (ISBN 0-553-29480-6) $3.50.
Walker, 1991. 128p. Hardbound (ISBN 0-8027-6993-4) $13.95. **Grades 5–12. 3Q, 2P.**

The next time you reach into the sugar bowl for a spoonful of sugar, think of Norbert Rilieux. As you wait for the traffic light to change at the next crosswalk, remember the name Garrett Morgan. They were inventors whose inventions changed our lives.

Norbert Rilieux was a brilliant engineer from Louisiana. In 1843 he developed a system for refining sugar that revolutionized the sugar industry. His system made it safer and more economical to produce sugar. He became wealthy, well-known, and respected, but was nevertheless denied many of his rights because he was black. In 1854, he was even required by law to carry a pass to allow him to travel freely in the city of New Orleans.

Garrett Morgan was born in Kentucky in 1875. He invented the traffic signals we see and take for granted every day, and received $40,000 from General Electric for his work. But not all of his inventions were accepted. One of his earlier inventions, a gas inhalator, helped save the lives of dozens of men trapped in a tunnel five miles out from shore and 282 feet under the icy waters of Lake Erie. Many people were impressed by Garrett's gas inhalator, and fire companies saw it as a valuable tool for improving their world. Many were ready to order the device, but when they found out that the inventor was black, they canceled their orders.

These are only two of the black inventors who changed our lives and our society. Meet the rest in *Outward Dreams: Black Inventors and Their Inventions*.

—*Kathleen Ellis*
Berkeley Carroll School, Brooklyn, NY

📖 Presenting Robert Cormier

Patricia J. Campbell. Nonfiction. Twayne,
1989. 189p. Hardbound (ISBN 0-8057-8212-5) $19.95 **Grades 7–12, adults. 4Q, 2P.**

In *The Chocolate War*, the first of Bob Cormier's young adult novels, Jerry Renault wonders if he dares to disturb his universe and challenge the evil that rules his high school. He dares, and his universe crumbles around him. But he isn't the only one of Cormier's characters to dare to challenge the establishment and the world he lives in. And just as in real life, the good guys don't always win. Good is only sometimes stronger than evil.

So what kind of a person would create *The Chocolate War*, a book so dark that when it was made into a movie, it was given a happy ending? What kind of man conjures up a person like Adam Farmer, on a never-ending search for his lost past? Who would bring to life a boy who could fade from sight, and make it so credible that you somehow have to believe it could be the truth?

Let me introduce you to Robert Cormier, Bob as his friends call him—and he has many. He is short and slight, with silvery hair and a smile that immediately makes even the most nervous fan relax. He frequently has insomnia, and for years was up writing when his kids got home from dates. He says, "There are things that can be said in those early morning hours that can be said at no other time."

Bob takes his stories from things that he himself has lived, like the school chocolate sale in *The Chocolate War*. He watched his ninth-grade son walk into the high school with two large sacks of candy, about to tell the school principal that he wouldn't sell candy in the school chocolate sale, and Bob said to himself, "What if . . . ?" There's a family reunion picture in Bob's family, with one gap in the top row, where all the young men were standing. Someone had ducked out of sight just as the photographer snapped the picture—or had he? Once again, Bob asked himself, "What if . . . ?" and Paul Theroux of *Fade* was created.

Bob is a person with a deep sense of what's right. When he was writing *I Am the Cheese*, he worried about what phone number to put in it as the number Adam dialed, trying to reach Amy. It was only the second book he'd written for teenagers, but he already knew his audience. "They'll know if I put in a fake number—they always start with 555—and if they can't trust me about that, how will they trust me to tell them the truth in the rest of the book?" So he put in his own phone number, and for years, when the phone rang, it was frequently for Amy. Bob's wife and kids quickly learned to ask those callers if they would like to speak to Amy's father, and soon they were talking to Bob himself. Not all of those calls were brief, and not all of them came at convenient times, but Bob always took the time to talk to the teenager on the other end of the line. "If they are desperate enough to call," he told me once, "the least I can to is take a few minutes to talk to them."

Take a few minutes to meet the man behind the books, to discover who he is and why he writes what he does. If you've ever wondered about how and why he creates those characters and situations that make you laugh, or cry, or scream with frustration, here are some of your answers. Let me present Robert Cormier.

—*JRB*

[Booktalks on the other titles in the Twayne Young Adult Author series will appear in the next issue of *NBT*—Ed.]

📖 Red Cap

G. Clifton Wisler. Lodestar Books, 1991.
160p. Hardbound (ISBN 0-525-67337-7)
$14.95. **Grades 5–8. 4Q, 2P.**

If you're 13 and only four feet tall, you can bet that the Army doesn't want you. But Ransom Powell just plain lied about his age, and joined the U.S. Army in 1862. He'd seen the scars on the back of a runaway slave, so he knew he had to fight for the North, even though two of his best friends had become Confederates and died in battle. So Ranse became a drummer boy, in charge of getting Company I up in the morning and calling them to meals and six other parts of their daily schedule, as well as beating out the captain's orders during drills and battles. [Optional: Show picture of a Civil War drummer boy. Two sources are: *The Battle of Gettysburg* by Neil Johnson (Four Winds, 1989), page 3; or *Tenting Tonight* by James I. Robertson, Jr. (Time Life, 1984), pages 18–19.]

The other soldiers kidded him a lot because of his small size, until Ranse learned how to play lots of practical jokes, which helped stop the teasing and improve company morale. He also learned that soldiers are always either too hot or too cold, and how to steal to improve the Army rations. And because the Civil War was the country's bloodiest, Ranse learned a lot about death and injury.

But it was a place, not an event, that made Ranse into a man. It was the infamous Camp Sumpter at Andersonville, Georgia, where the only shelter was rigged from scraps and rags, and food was almost nonexistent. [Optional: Show picture of the camp from *Tenting Tonight*, pages 130–31.]

To find out why Ranse turned down a chance to get out of Andersonville, and how he survived when hundreds around him were dying, read *Red Cap*.

—*Willa Jean Harner*
Tiffin-Seneca Public Library, Tiffin, OH

Presenting YA Authors

By Patty Campbell, General Editor, Twayne Young Adult author series; columnist, *Wilson Library Bulletin*; avocado rancher

In November 1982, Ron Brown, the Young Adult Coordinator for Boston Public Library, made me an offer I couldn't refuse. He wrote, "I am inviting you to be the first contributor to an important series of critical volumes to be published by Twayne, a division in G. K. Hall, in which each book will be devoted to the life and work of one young adult author." I could have any writer, he said, *anybody*. Like any sensible critic, I pounced on Robert Cormier, and spent the next two years happily analyzing the rich, complex layers of his novels and getting to know the kind, sunny man who is the author of those dark stories.

In November 1985, the series was launched with a gala party at the Harvard Bookstore Cafe, at which Bob and I signed copies of "our" book. Many people felt that the occasion, 21 years after the publication of *The Outsiders*, also marked the coming of age of adolescent literature. Serious critical attention was now being paid to a genre that had been considered lightweight by those who had not read any of the fine writers who had appeared in the field during the last two decades.

Under Ron Brown's capable guidance, works on those writers began to appear as volumes in the Twayne Young Adult Authors series: *Presenting M. E. Kerr, Presenting Norma Fox Mazer, Presenting Rosa Guy*, and so on. In 1987, pressures of work forced Ron to resign, and again I was made an offer I couldn't refuse—I took over as General Editor. Twayne's Athenaide Dallett and I worked together with much mutual joy and respect, shaping the series carefully. Later, when she left to continue her education at Harvard, Elizabeth Fowler became in-house editor. After her, Carol Chin took on the job. Sylvia Miller currently fills the position. All four women have brought to their work a dedication to excellence and a love of YA literature. Last year Twayne became an imprint of Macmillan, and the editorial offices were moved from Boston to New York, but the company continues to maintain a strong commitment to the series.

As editor of the series, I have been responsible for its style and content. An ongoing stylistic challenge is the fact that the books are aimed at dual audiences with very different needs and expectations: first, teachers and librarians and second, young adults themselves. From the very first, I was concerned that the books be "lively," a quality we defined as readability, gutsiness, warmth, and openness to audacity and surprise. In my own book on Cormier, I even snuck in Connie Cormier's recipe for chocolate almond mousse, as a test of Twayne's commitment to liveliness. (They passed, so I took it out in the updated edition.) Maryann Weidt's introduction to *Presenting Judy Blume*, in which she shares her emotions as a bumbling Midwesterner in Judy Blume's elegant New York penthouse, is an even better example. For the sake of vivid portraiture, I often send writers back to describe their subjects' living rooms, find out what kind of cars they drive, or learn the names of their pets. [Patty doesn't mention her own introduction to *Presenting Robert Cormier*, which vividly re-creates a bicycle ride on a snowy New England night. Knowing that she grew up in Los Angeles, is overwhelmed with excitement at even the slightest frosting of snow, and doesn't even know how to ride a bike, I immediately called her and demanded to know how she knew so much about riding a bike in the snow, because she'd gotten it exactly right. She told me her husband had explained it to her. Patty not only knows how to elicit vivid portraits, she knows how to write them as well!—**Ed**.]

For teachers and librarians we try to provide a serious traditional literary analysis of each author's work, with attention to plot structure, theme, character, and imagery. But we also try to delve deeper into the creative process, by tracking down early drafts or unpublished manuscripts, by consulting with editors or other mentors, and by examining influences in literature, film, or social movements. Teachers have welcomed the series as an invaluable aid to teaching young adult literature in depth. Librarians have also been enthusiastic about being able to offer young researchers an attractive, accessible resource for information about their favorite authors. Also, many librarians tell us that the series is enormously helpful as a booktalk tool, not only for plot summaries and character definitions, but also for interesting background anecdotes and answers to puzzling questions like, "Who was Mr. Grey *really*?"

Although the general format is the same, the individual volumes are uniquely shaped by their subjects, and each brings a uniquely useful perspective to the classroom. *Presenting William Sleator*, for example, records the intense and often painful dialogue between author and editor as a novel takes shape in a mutual creative process. *Presenting Zibby Oneal* examines the earlier, unpublished versions of her books and the careful changes in them that result in this author's perfection of style. *Presenting Walter*

Dean Myers takes a broad historical view of Afro-American traditions in language and folklore as they appear in that author's work. *Presenting Robert Cormier* initiates young critics into the joys of deconstruction, and reveals the hidden jewels to be found in a literary archaeological dig.

One of the most challenging aspects of my job as General Editor is to find the perfect biographer for each author. I look first for persons who can write and who have a track record in published literary criticism. The second essential qualification is expertise in young adult literature and a consequent reputation in the field. After that, my work really begins. I look for compatible personalities and shared interests. The person who writes about Paula Danziger, for instance, must adore sushi and shopping and be willing at least to pretend to love pinball, in addition to being warm and unstuffy and a good audience for one-liners. Gary Paulsen's biographer needs to have pine needles in his sleeping bag. And then I try to match styles. The cool, quiet tone of Susan Bloom and Cathryn Mercier's *Presenting Zibby Oneal* exactly fits their subject.

Right now we have 14 titles in print (see the following list) and as many more in the works. Our latest, *Presenting Young Adult Horror Fiction* by Dr. Cosette Kies, is something of a departure from our usual pattern, in that it examines a whole genre rather than a single author. Other genre studies in process are *Presenting Young Adult Fantasy*, by Cathi Dunn MacRae, and *Presenting Young Adult Science Fiction*, by Janice Antczak. Our newest individual author study, *Presenting Madeleine L'Engle*, is currently in production. Other single-author studies now under contract include books on Lois Duncan, Chris Crutcher, Harry Mazer, Cynthia Voigt, Lynn Hall, Ouida Subestyen, Laurence Yep, Gary Paulsen, and Paula Danziger. And there are many more to come, as long as young adult literature continues.

The Twayne Young Adult Authors Series

Presenting Judy Blume, Maryann N. Weidt.

Presenting Sue Ellen Bridgers, by Ted Hipple.

Presenting Robert Cormier (updated ed.), by Patricia J. Campbell.

Presenting Rosa Guy, by Jerrie Norris.

Presenting S. E. Hinton (updated ed.), by Jay Daly.

Presenting M. E. Kerr, by Alleen Pace Nilsen.

Presenting Norma Klein, by Allene Stuart Phy.

Presenting Norma Fox Mazer, by Sally Holmes Holtze.

Presenting Walter Dean Myers, by Rudine Sims Bishop.

Presenting Richard Peck, by Donald R. Gallo.

Presenting Paul Zindel, by Jack Jacob Forman.

Presenting Zibby Oneal, by Susan P. Bloom and Cathryn M. Mercier.

Presenting William Sleator, by James E. Davis and Hazel K. Davis.

Presenting Young Adult Horror Fiction, by Cosette Kies.

(Dell also publishes these titles in paperback.)

[I have just received review copies of these titles, and talks on them will appear in the next issue (Fall 1993) of *NBT*—**Ed.**]

Poetry

All the Colors of the Race

Arnold Adoff. Illustrated by John Steptoe. Beech Tree Books, 1992. 56p. Paperbound (ISBN 0-688-11496-2) $4.95. Lothrop, 1982. 56p. Hardbound (ISBN 0-688-00879-8) $12.95. **Grades 5–12, adults. 3Q, 2P.**

All the colors of the race
are
in my face . . . .
The human race, where
there is every shade
of brown, and tan,
and paler
honey,
creamy gold . . . .

I am a mixture that makes me unique—my father is white, my mother is black, and I am both Jewish and Protestant. Listen to my story in my poetry, as I tell you what it's like to have the blood of two races running through my veins, the heritage of two religions in my mind.

I am making a circle for my self
I am making a circle for my self and
I am placing into that
circle: all who are for me, and all that is inside . . . .
Come into my circle and know who I am.

—Anna B. Hart
Sherwood Regional Library,
Fairfax County Public Library, Alexandria, VA

And the Green Grass Grew All Around: Folk Poetry from Everyone

Alvin Schwartz. Illustrated by Sue Truesdell. HarperCollins, 1992. 193p. Hardbound (ISBN 0-06-022757-5) $15.00. **Grades 3–6. 4Q, 3P.** Reviewed in: Bklst, 5/1/92, p. 1598; HB, 7/8/92, p. 460; SLJ, 6/92, p. 135.

[This talk is intended for an adult audience—**Ed.**]

Boom, boom, ain't it great to be crazy,
Boom, boom, ain't it great to be crazy,
To be silly and foolish the whole day through,
Boom, boom, ain't it great to be crazy.
A horse and a flea and three blind mice
Sat on a curbstone shooting dice,
The horse said "Oops," and fell on the flea,
And the flea said "Whoops, there's a horsey on me!"

Ah, the memories of summer camp, where after dinner we'd all gather around the campfire and sing nonsense songs and chant rhymes about people, food, and school. This collection is guaranteed to make those memories live again. Curl up in a comfortable chair and browse through over 250 folk poems, just begging to be shared with children and grandchildren. It's a wonderful trip down memory lane. How many of you can finish this one?

On top of spaghetti
All covered with cheese . . . .

[This talk is intended for children—Ed.]

How many of you have gone to summer camp? Do you remember some of the songs you sang, maybe on the bus on the way there or after dinner, around the campfire? Funny, silly songs that really didn't make any sense, but they made you laugh just the same? Did you sing this one?

On top of spaghetti
All covered with cheese,
I lost my poor meatball
When somebody sneezed.

This book has lots of these nonsense rhymes and songs, maybe some you know and some you don't. Maybe next summer you can be the one to come up with a new song to sing and laugh about around the campfire. Maybe even this one:

Boom, boom, ain't it great to be crazy,
Boom, boom, ain't it great to be crazy,
To be silly and foolish the whole day through,
Boom, boom, ain't it great to be crazy.

—Mary Ann Capan
Western Illinois University, Macomb, IL

Aska's Animals

David Day. Illustrated by Warabe Aska. Doubleday, 1991. 32p. Hardbound (ISBN 0-385-25315-X) $15.00. **Grades 3–12, adults. 4Q, 4P.**

Have you ever wondered, "Where did the animals come from? What god or spirit shaped them?" The two men who created this book wondered about it, too. For them, "It's a guessing game . . . Imagining how the beasts began."

What kinds of beginnings did they imagine? [Show illustrations from the book at appropriate places (page numbers are noted in brackets throughout this talk), or choose other animals as examples if you prefer.]

Perhaps the "first horses were made of sea foam . . ." [p. 5], the first deer were "tree spirits . . . restless for flight . . ." [p. 7], the first camels "shaped by the lovely song/Of the wind whispering over shifting sands" [p. 13]. But the hippopotamuses are easy to imagine [p. 17]—

There can be no doubt about hippopotamuses,
Those happy, lazy, yawning monsters.
Shaped out of great lumps of muck by
childish gods,
Then left to bake in the sun.
Hippos are monuments to the glories of mud.

These are just a few of the wonderful animals whose beginnings are imagined in this book, and the authors invite all of us to join them in naming more, because, after all,

The world is wide and full of wonders,
Imagining beginnings is a never-ending game.

—*Olivia Jacobs*
Wichita Heights High School, Wichita, KS

📖 At the Crack of the Bat

Compiled by Lillian Morrison. Illustrated by Steve Cieslawski. Hyperion, 1992. 64p. Hardbound (ISBN 1-56282-177-6) $14.95. **Grades 5–8. 4Q, 3P.**

You probably haven't ever thought of baseball and poetry as having a lot in common—but to some poets, they do. Poets who describe the game they love and the players they admire: Nolan Ryan, José Canseco, Babe Ruth, Jackie Robinson, and others. For people who really love baseball, sometimes it takes a poem to describe it. Plain words alone may not be able to convey the pleasure and the pain, but somehow a poem can sing out loudly and clearly. Listen to one poet's "Analysis of Baseball":

It's about
the ball,
the bat,
and the mitt.
Ball hits
bat, or it
hits mitt.

Another poet advises:

If at first you don't succeed,
Slide for second.

My advice to you is: Don't miss this book—it's a home run!

—*Bette D. Ammon*
Missoula Public Library, Missoula, MT

📖 The Ice Cream Store

Dennis Lee. Illustrated by David McPhail. Scholastic, 1992. 64p. Hardbound (ISBN 0-590-45861-2) $14.95. **Grades 3–4. 4Q, 4P.**

Oh, the kids around the block are like an
Ice cream store,
'Cause there's chocolate and vanilla,
And there's maple and there's more,
And there's butterscotch and orange—
Yes, there's flavors by the score;
And the kids around the block are like an
Ice cream store!

These poems are like an ice cream store, too, because they're about kids from all over the world. Ever dig a hole to Australia? Well, some kids in this book do.

We're digging a hole to Australia,
But it's kind of going slow.
And we've got some juice and cookies,
But they're getting kind of low.

They're eating as fast as they're digging, so they're worried about the kids in Australia being willing to share with them, because it looks like, by the time they get to Australia, they'll have eaten all the food they'd planned to share with their new friends.

Did you hear about Mrs. Mitchell's underwear?

Mrs. Mitchell's underwear
Is dancing on the line;
Mrs. Mitchell's underwear
Has never looked so fine.
Mrs. Mitchell hates to dance—
She says it's not refined,
But Mrs. Mitchell's underwear
Is prancing on the line.

Mrs. Mitchell may not like to dance, but her underwear sure does!

Do you know what a fib is? Have you ever seen one grow?

I found a fib on Friday
In a pile of styrofoam.
It looked so cute and cuddly
I just had to bring it home.
It was a teeny, tiny fib,

It's true—
Till the darn thing grew!

There's going to be trouble here—always is, when a fib grows, you know.

You'll meet Stinky from Helsinki, and discover Skinny marinka dinka—and guess what it is! Do you know how to get rid of Chillybones? Have you ever eaten gumbo till you know your "belly's gonna blast apart" or traveled in a rocket ship or had a Martian visit you? You can do all those things in the poems in this book. But be careful when you meet Big Bad Billy—he's the guy that pulled his belly button out!

—**Maggie Carey**
The Barstow School, Kansas City, MO

In the Eyes of the Cat: Japanese Poetry for All Seasons

Selected and illustrated by Demi. Translated by Tze-Si Huang. Holt, 1992. Unpaged. Hardcover (ISBN 0-8050-1955-3) $25.95. **Grades 5–12, adults. 4Q, 2P.**

In the eyes of the cat
Is the color of the sea
On a sunny day, in winter.

Japanese haiku, poems that reflect the beauty of our world in only a few syllables, create a picture that freezes a moment in time, so we can enjoy it over and over again. These poems show the passing of the seasons, the cycle of nature, and the places and purposes of the insects, flowers, and animals that are a part of it.

A mother horse
Keeps watch
While her child
Drinks.

Discover the beauty and complexity of this place we call our home.

—**Anna B. Hart**
Sherwood Regional Library,
Fairfax County Public Library, Alexandria, VA

Judy Scuppernong

Brenda Seabrooke. Illustrated by Ted Lewin. Bantam, 1992. 64p. Paperbound (ISBN 0-533-29448-2) $3.50. Dutton, 1990. 64p. Hardbound (ISBN 0-525-65038-5) $12.95. **Grades 7–12. 3Q, 2P.**

I'll never forget the summer I was 10. It was the summer of Judy Scuppernong. Eustacia, Laura Louise, and I had always been a threesome, but that summer, after Judy Scuppernong came to town, we were four.

Judy was different and exotic in a way that was hard to explain. She wore her long, pale hair straight with bangs—not in ponytails, braids, or curls, like we did—and she painted her toenails bright red.

Our mothers had forbidden us to go inside Judy's house, so we gathered in her back yard. There was no sign of Judy's father, and we never saw her mother, just shadows behind the window shades. There was a glass house with a stone floor in Judy's back yard. She called it her greenhouse. The floor was covered with a layer of broken glass that seemed to get deeper as the summer went on. But where did the glass come from? No one ever knew.

The summer was almost over when I went to Judy's house alone one day, and discovered the secret of the glass house. And one day not long after that, Judy was gone— vanished, like a puff of smoke. And so the summer of my tenth year was over and I was innocent no more.

—**Mary Ann Capan**
Western Illinois University, Macomb, IL

Monster Soup and Other Spooky Poems

Compiled by Dilys Evans. Illustrated by Jacqueline Rogers. Scholastic, 1992. 40p. Hardcover (ISBN 0-590-45208-8) $14.95. **Grades 3–6. 4Q, 4P.**

Here's a riddle for you:
What night would it be?
If the moon shines
On black pines
And an owl flies,
And a ghost cries
And the hairs rise
on the back
on the back on the back of your neck—

What night would it be? Why, Halloween, of course! And when a witch's little girl goes to bed on Halloween night, she wants a special bedtime story:

"Tell me a story,"
Says Witch's Child.
"About the Beast
So fierce and wild.
About a Ghost
That shrieks and groans.
A Skeleton
That rattles bones.
About a Monster
Crawly-creepy.
Something nice
To make me sleepy!"

But watch out, little Witch—did you know there's something hiding under your bed?

Tonight is the night
When dead leaves fly
Like witches on switches
Across the sky,
When elf and sprite
Flit through the night
On a moony sheen . . . .
Tonight is the night
When pumpkins stare
Through sheaves and leaves
Everywhere,
When ghoul and ghost
And goblin host
Dance 'round their queen.
It's Halloween!

But there's more than Halloween to be found here—all kinds of other creatures, from dragons to dinosaurs, from monsters to mice, stroll or prowl, cavort or dance, and all just for you!

—*JRB*

📖 Polaroids and Other Points of View

Betsy Hearne. Photographs by Peter Kiar. Macmillan, 1991. 68p. Hardbound (ISBN 0-689-50530-2) $12.95. **Grades 9–12, adults. 4Q, 1P.**

Poems can create small snapshots of nature, the city, people, senses, dreams, and time, like this one called "Babysitting":

We were watching "Sesame Street" one day
when everything turned around
busses backing
rain rising
city slowing down.
We rushed to the east to go to the beach
The lake was filled with sand
fish walking
people barking
the water felt dry to my hand.
We went downtown to the city zoo
they locked us up in a cage
an elephant
and a wolf walked by—
I stared back in a rage.
We walked outside to the city park
where pigeons drove cars by.
The kid I was sitting
jumped off her swing
and flew into the sky.
Over the playground,

running to climb.
a shooting star spun round.
but once in a while
kids' feet forget
to catch them coming down.
And then the land
seems a sad man
and the sky is surprised by it all.

But a poem doesn't always need a lot of words to create a picture:

Spring whispers secret
rain to the listening trees
till they shout loud green.

These are only two of the poems you'll discover here—read them and create your own instant pictures.

—*Faye A. Powell*
Prince George's County Memorial Library,
District Heights, MD

📖 Shades of Green

Compiled by Anne Harvey. Illustrated by John Lawrence. Macmillan, 1992. 192p. Hardbound (ISBN 0-688-10890-3) $18.00. **Grades 5–12, adults. 3Q, 1P.**

What is green?
Green is the grass
And the leaves of the trees
Green is the smell
Of a country breeze . . .

There are green shades in every one of these poems—green grasshoppers and crickets, green pickles, green weeds, green birds, green lizards, and even green eyes. Do you ever think about all the things in nature that are green? There's lots of green around now, but how long will we be able to see it?

As asphalt and concrete
Replace bushes and trees,
As highways and buildings
Replace marshes and woods,
What will replace
The song of the birds?

And the little boy asks, "Why did they knock down all the trees, Daddy?"

Nowhere to play;
Backstreets and alleyways,
Car-parks and main roads;
Noise, dirt, and danger all day.
Same old noises;
Rush of traffic,

Cops on their way;
Where's the ice-cream man today?

"I didn't want anything new—just a place to play,"
says the boy.

No new sensations;
Same hard pavements,
No mud to explore.
No pebbles, no pieces of wood to arrange.
Big buildings,
Big buses, big people;
No bee on a buttercup,
No ants on their way.
No green grass, just concrete,
No thrush song, just sirens.
Seasons passing unnoticed;
Nowhere to play—"What's on telly today?"

Do these poems remind you about taking care of our planet, of Earth Day? Can you imagine what the world would be like if there were no open spaces, no green country?

Green trees are also remembrances of special people—trees are planted so that their memories will live on. Wes Magee writes about Tracy's tree. She was a special friend who was run over and killed. Wes remembers that just last year, Tracy was here and the tree was not.

Last year it was not there,
the sapling with purplish leaves
planted in our school grounds with care.
It's Tracy's tree, my friend who died,
and last year it was not there.

—Maggie Carey
The Barstow School, Kansas City, MO

📖 Sisters of the Earth

Loraine Anderson. Random, 1991. 426p. Hardbound (ISBN 0-679-73382-5) $13.00. Adults. 4Q, 1P.

"He says that women speak with nature. That she hears voices from under the earth . . . . He says he is not part of this world, that he was set on this world as a stranger. We are the bird's eggs, . . . we are sheep . . . we are leaves of ivy . . . . We are women. We rise with the wave. We are gazelle . . . and peach . . . we are air, we are flame . . . we are girls. We are woman and nature. And he says he cannot hear us speak. But we hear."

These words by Susan Griffin describe this collection of women's prose and poetry on nature. Here you will find their feelings and observations on the wonders of animals, plants, the sky, and the waters, for they are the words of our sisters, our *Sisters of the Earth.*

—Faye A. Powell
Prince George's County Memorial Library, District Heights, MD

📖 Strawberry Drums

Edited by Adrian Mitchell. Delacorte, 1991. 38p. Hardbound (ISBN 0-385-30287-8) $13.95. **Grades 3–4. 3Q, 1P.**

Poetry began in the time when everybody
lived in tribes.
Some lived in caves, some lived in igloos,
some lived in huts on stilts or in smoky tents.
Some tribes were hunters, some tribes grew
their food.
But every tribe made up poems.
And their poems were usually sung and
danced.

Here you'll find poetry from all over the world, poetry that reflects the rhythm and the life of the people that wrote it, poetry that laughs, cries, and sometimes teaches a lesson. One poem is called "And God Said to the Little Boy." God asks the little boy if he ate "that there apple"—"No Lord," he says. Then God asks the little girl the same question, and gets the same answer.

Then the Lord pointed with his finger
And fixed them both with his stare,
And he said in a voice like a Rolls Royce
"Well, what are them two cores doing there?"

—Maggie Carey
The Barstow School, Kansas City, MO

📖 The Wacky Book of Witches

Annie Civardi. Illustrated by Graham Philpot. Scholastic, 1992. 32p. Hardcover (ISBN 0-590-45094-8) $14.95. **Grades 3–6. 4Q, 4P.**

What sort of folks would live in a place called Cackle Town? Why, bad, wacky witches, of course! The kind of witches who are scary, stingy, sneaky, mean . . . and yes—wacky! The sort of creepy and goofy witches who cast grisly spells and stir up ghastly concoctions of slimy slugs and turtle tongues with a pinch of viper venom and just a splash of coffin syrup. So—welcome to Cackle Town. You won't want to miss the grubby Halloween party at Old Warty's Tower—all children will be eaten! But be sure to avoid the Grewsome Gardens and Broomstick Park. And keep far, far away from Abracadabra Alley and the Charmless Lotta, or perhaps, Jocasta Spell.

—Bette D. Ammon
Missoula Public Library, Missoula, MT

📖 The Word Party

Richard Edwards. Illustrated by John
Lawrence. Delacorte, 1992. 72p. Hardbound
(ISBN 0-385-30620-2) $13.50. **Grades 5–12.**
4Q, 2P.

[Create a prop: an invitation in an envelope with the
word *YOU* written on the outside. Open it and read.]

You are invited to a word party. Bring your own words
if you wish, but be prepared to celebrate with the
man of many brushes, Lily who dances, Daisy who hides,
Rosie who paints, and the unnamed, untamed beast. Don't
be alarmed by Uncle Fazackerly's sneezes, lunging shapes
from the murky pond, or the monster in the woods whose
breath makes bushes die. And remember—it's a word
party, so the guests are words and poems and YOU. Big
Bert will be there too. You'll recognize him right away:

> Big Bert sat on a cushion,
> "I'm much too fat," moaned he.
> "Who else could be so miserable?"
> And the cushion answered "Me!"

> —*Bette D. Ammon*
> Missoula Public Library, Missoula, MT

Short Story and Drama Collections

📖 Center Stage: One Act Plays for Teenage Readers and Actors

Edited by Donald R. Gallo. HarperCollins, 1990. 362p. Hardbound (ISBN 0-06-022170-4) $16.95. **Grades 7–12, adults. 4Q, 3P.**

When is a short story not a short story? When it's a play. When is a play not dull and boring to read—or to perform? When it's written by an author who has already written books for teenagers. The plays in this collection are not dull and boring—they are funny, or sad, or mysterious, and all of them show what it's like to be a teenager. If you liked Don Gallo's short story collections (*Sixteen, Visions, Connections*), I'm sure you'll like reading plays by some of the authors from his other books.

For instance, "Driver's Test" by Alden Carter. Ben is awkward, clumsy, and is always falling over his own feet, or breaking and spilling everything he touches. He is also trying to get his driver's license. He's already failed his driving test once, and the second time he goes to take it, he pulls out of the lot, signals right, and turns left. It's a new world's record for failing. To make matters worse, he's just asked the prettiest girl in school, Debbie Byers, on a date. And because she is the prettiest girl in school, when Debbie goes out on a date, she does not expect to have to walk any further than from the front door to the car. Is there any way that Ben can save both his face and his date?

But not all of these plays are funny. They're also about suicide, popularity, divorce, dating, romance, and school. Jeremy is right in the middle of his parents' fights and can't figure out how to get out. His dad is always late with his child support checks, and Jeremy's mother sends him to get the check. But when Jeremy comes back without it, his mother gets mad at *him*, not his father. Rick takes aerobics because his brother told him it was a great place to meet girls. It's true that the room is full of gorgeous girls in leotards. The only problem is that they're all laughing at him because he's falling all over himself trying to follow the instructor.

And that's only a few of the people you'll meet when you discover what's going on at *Center Stage*.

—Susan Dunn
Salem Public Library, Salem, OR

📖 Colors of a New Day

Sarah Lefanu and Stephen Hayward. Pantheon, 1990. 397p. Hardbound (ISBN 0-679-73094-X) $12.95. **Grades 9–12, adults. 4Q, 1P.**

We do not exist in a vacuum, nor is each of us completely alone. The fate on the human race rests equally on all of our shoulders. The struggles of a people half a world away are just as relevant to us as the conflicts we have in our own cities and homes. That's only one of the reasons why this book is important. The stories and poems in it were collected to help support the African National Congress in its efforts to bring equality to South Africa. They were written by natives of Africa, North America, Asia, Great Britain, and the Caribbean. Joyce Carol Oates makes you stop and think in "Black," James Kilman helps you smile with understanding as you read "Lassies Are Trained that Way," and Vikram Seth may bring tears to your eyes with "Biko," a short poem that shouts to you about the death of a peaceful freedom fighter.

Nelson Mandela's foreword says that this book was published to raise the consciousness of the world. Take a look at it, and see the *Colors of a New Day* shine brightly.

—Faye A. Powell
Prince George's Memorial Library System, District Heights, MD

📖 A Couple of Kooks and Other Stories about Love

Cynthia Rylant. Dell, 1990. 104p. Paperbound (ISBN 0-440-21210-3) $3.50. **Grades 5–12, adults. 4Q, 3P.**

This book is only for people who like love stories. Love stories that make you laugh, love stories that make you cry, love stories that make you wish you were in love or glad that you are.

Ernie and Dolores are only two of the people you'll meet in this book. Ernie is mentally handicapped, and for 31 years he lived alone with his mother, shut up in a dark house, never allowed to go to school or play with other children. But when his mother died suddenly, Ernie was thrust into the world he'd never been a part of before.

He was moved to a nearby group home, where he was so frightened that he clung to his beloved box of flower seeds and stayed in his room alone. Gradually, he was coaxed out of his shell by one of the workers, who loved gardening and helped Ernie plant his seeds and care for the plants that grew from them. They also started going out to breakfast once a week, early in the morning before it got too crowded and frightening for Ernie. It was in the diner that Ernie fell in love with Dolores.

Dolores was the only woman in town who worked in a hardware store and the only woman in town with a tattoo. Because of that, most people never thought about Dolores being someone who could be loved and love in return—she was so "unfeminine." But to Ernie, she was perfect. Early every Wednesday morning, he collected handfuls of his precious flowers and put them in a Mason jar. He left the jar of flowers just in front of the entrance to the hardware store before it opened for business. Everyone teased Dolores about her mystery boyfriend, but no one ever suspected that it was Ernie. The flowers made Dolores feel happy and attractive, and Ernie was happy because she was and because he was able to give something wonderful to someone he loved.

Those are only two of the lovers you'll meet in this book, including the kooks from the title story, talking to their unborn baby, explaining to it who its parents were, even though it would never meet them.

Laugh and cry as you read, and then share these stories with someone you love.

—Susan R. Farber
Ossining Public Library, Ossining, NY

A Fit of Shivers

Joan Aiken. Delacorte, 1992. 144p. Hardbound (ISBN 0-385-30691-1) $15.00. **Grades 7–12. 3Q, 3P.**

When the old man dreamed, the dog whined. Out in the remote cottage, the boy lived with his grandfather and his dog Flag. The days went well, but the nights did not. They were worse than the days, worse than death.

The old man told his grandson, "Night is a kind of death. You know that I have bad dreams." The old man's dreams were terrible to hear. He would yell and scream, toss and turn, sometimes hurling himself right off the bed and onto the floor. And the entire time he was having the bad dream, the dog Flag would whine as he sat at the foot of the stairs listening to the old man's terror in the night.

The boy asked him what the bad dreams were about, but all the old man would say was, "Something." Something so horrible, so terrible, so terrifying that it had no name. The something that was the worst thing of all. And then one day, the old man died. They took the body to the church. The boy was sad. Flag just lay in the old man's bedroom like a stone, not moving an inch. Then, three nights after the old man died, Flag jumped up and took off running. The boy yelled after him, but the dog was gone.

The next morning, the boy went to the church to see his grandfather's body one last time before they lowered it into the ground. When he walked into the room where his grandfather's body had been laid out, what he saw froze his blood. His grandfather's body was no longer where it had been placed. It lay on the floor, and next to it was Flag, whining. It had been one last bad dream, one last encounter with something, something so horrible, so terrible, so terrifying that it had no name. The something that was the worst thing of all.

And that's just one of the stories that will give you *A Fit of Shivers.*

—Patrick Jones
Allen County Public Library, Fort Wayne, IN

Hauntings: Ghosts and Ghouls from Around the World

Margaret Hodges. Illustrated by David Wenzel. Little, Brown, 1991. 123p. Hardbound (ISBN 0-316-36796-6) $16.95. **Grades 5–8. 3Q, 4P.**

How would you like to have Death for a godfather? That's what happened to one man. When he was born, his father ran out into the road to find a godfather for his son. As he ran along, Death came striding up to him. "Let me be your boy's godfather," he said, and the man agreed. Death told the man that his son would be rich and famous, and would lack for nothing, for anyone who had Death as a friend was very lucky indeed. When the boy grew up, he became a famous physician, for his godfather told him which people would live or die, and gave him an herb that would heal the sick.

One day the doctor was asked to heal a king who had fallen gravely ill. When the doctor arrived, he saw Death standing at the king's feet, a sure sign that the man would die. But the doctor decided that the king should live, and gave him some of the magic herb. Death was very angry, and said, "Since you are my godson, I will pardon you. But defy me again and it will cost your life." Soon after, the king's daughter became ill, and when the physician saw her, he fell in love with her because she was so beautiful. Even though Death stood nearby, he saved the princess. But he had to pay the price. He had defied Death twice, and Death had his vengeance. The doctor fell dead at the princess's side.

If you love stories of ghouls and ghosts and goblins, then this is the book for you. You'll find tales filled with rattling bones, the tolling of unseen bells, and voices pleading for mercy or screaming in fear. For those of you who don't mind wakeful nights and have a working night light, try *Hauntings: Ghosts and Ghouls from Around the World.*

—*Nancy A. Weitendorf*
Oxford Lane Library, Oxford, OH

📖 Larger Than Life

Robert D. San Souci. Illustrated by Andrew Glass. Doubleday, 1991. 59p. Hardbound (ISBN 0-385-24907-1) $16.00. **Grades 3–8. 4Q, 3P.**

I'd like to introduce you to five larger-than-life heroes. They're stronger, braver, and more adventuresome than anyone you're likely to meet these days.

You might already have heard of John Henry. Some folks say he weighed 44 pounds the night he was born. This black giant stood up to the newly invented steam drill that belonged to the owners of the C&O Railroad.

Then get to know Alfred Bulltop Stormalong, the greatest Yankee sailor of New England's tall ships. As a boy, sometimes Stormy swam the hundred miles or more from Maine to Cape Cod just for a little fun. You'll follow his adventures around the world—even his trip to Italy, where he leaned against the Tower of Pisa. It's been leaning ever since.

Slue-foot Sue could whistle so loud that people in the next state reached for teakettles that weren't even on the fire. Her wedding to Pecos Bill was talked about for years afterward.

And shake hands with Texas hero Strap Buckner, who could never turn down a fight—even with the Devil himself. "Skin for skin!" said the Devil, and Strap found himself in the contest of his life.

Finally, you'll meet Paul Bunyan, who dug the Great Lakes just so that Babe, his blue ox, would always have fresh water. Join their adventures in the Dakotas and the Pacific Northwest.

These people are bigger, taller, better, braver. They're our American folk heroes, and you can meet them all.

—*Anna B. Hart*
Sherwood Regional Library, Fairfax County Library System,
Alexandria, VA

📖 Nightwaves: Scary Tales for After Dark

Collin McDonald. HarperCollins, 1992. 112p. Paperbound (ISBN 0-06-440447-1) $3.95. Dutton, 1990. 112p. Hardbound (ISBN 0-525-65043-1) $12.95. **Grades 5–12. 4Q, 4P.**

Janet always looked forward to each spring with both anticipation and dread. School was almost over, the gray chill of winter was giving way to warm sunshine—but it was also the time that her mother planted the garden.

Janet and her mother lived all alone after her father died, and the garden was her mother's main source of comfort. She loved each one of the tiny plants that grew up to produce all kinds of flowers, and each year the garden got a little bigger.

Janet hated the garden. She hated the time she had to spend on it, planting, watering, weeding. She wanted to be with her friends, she wanted to be free. And she hated the way the garden seemed to be taking over their yard. Other people could admire it, and shower her mother with compliments. Janet hated it, and soon she hated her mother for making her work in it.

But what Janet didn't know was that the plants her mother grew were not your average garden-variety plants and flowers. And one night, Janet discovered just how much power those plants had over her, when she tried to destroy them.

The radio Tom built whispered the future to him. He knew all the headlines the day before they happened. Soon the media found out about it, and his picture was in all the papers. People began to call him and demand that he help them solve their problems or find their loved ones. There were far too many for him to help, and the excitement wore off quickly. Then, just as he was about to smash the radio so that everyone would let him alone, he had a wonderful thought—he could win thousands and thousands of dollars by betting on races and games whose outcomes he already knew. His brother told him it was cheating, but Tom wouldn't listen. Too bad he didn't listen to the radio just a little longer—maybe he wouldn't have run out into the street so fast that afternoon.

They said the dam was haunted, but by the time the fifth-grade class left that afternoon, it had two ghosts, not one. So what did Christine see when she went back to the dam for the first time since that day 25 years ago? Was it a ghost, or just her imagination? How real can a ghost be, anyway?

And next time you're out on a camping trip, remember the story about the crazed killer in the woods, and the handsome forest ranger who came to help a group of girls camping alone in the woods at night. There are people who are very different from what they seem to be—even when they look very good in uniform.

Those are only a few of the eight stories you'll find in this book, guaranteed to make you want to keep that light burning all night long. Nighty nightmare!

—*JRB*

📖 Railway Ghosts and Highway Horrors

Daniel Cohen. Illustrated by Stephen Marchesi. Cobblehill Books, 1991. 109p. Hardcover (ISBN 0-525-65071-7) $13.95. **Grades 5–12. 3Q, 4P.**

The car was gorgeous—and what a low price! Vince couldn't believe that they only wanted $1,000 for a Jaguar. But sure enough, the car salesman told him that was the price. Vince took it for a test drive. He was sure there had to be some hitch, but the car ran like a dream. Vince didn't even have to think twice—he bought it and drove it home immediately. The only problem was a sort of funny smell, but that was probably just the leather upholstery.

The neighbors were green with envy when they saw Vince's new car, and for a while it was great—just the car Vince had always wanted. But the funny smell kept getting worse and worse. Nothing Vince tried to get rid of it helped. And then he began to notice a face in the rear-view mirror . . . a man's face, a nasty face. It seemed to be watching him.

Finally Vince could stand it no more. He took the car back to the lot, and the salesman told him why the car had been for sale so cheap. It had once belonged to a big-time gangster. His associates thought he was double-crossing them, so they shot him and stuffed him in the trunk. Then they left the car in an airport parking lot. It had sat there for a month before the body was found. The car was eventually cleaned up and sold at a police auction, but the smell always came back. It seems that the gangster wanted to stay with his favorite automobile, and most people didn't care for the back-seat driver.

Roads, highways, railroad tracks. Not a day goes by that we don't travel down them, and sometimes, someone has a ghostly meeting as they travel. Is that strange shape by the side of the road a tree, or is it something else, something more sinister? If you want to travel with peace of mind, then don't read this book just before you leave . . . .

—Nancy A. Weitendorf
Oxford Lane Library, Oxford, OH

📖 Short Circuits

Edited by Donald R. Gallo. Delacorte, 1992. 224p. Hardcover (ISBN 0-385-30785-3) $16.00. **Grades 5–8. 3Q, 2P.**

I first noticed her standing in the doorway of the old abandoned house. The land and the house had been abandoned before I was born—over 16 years ago. Every-body said the place was haunted. I didn't believe in ghosts, not then, but I sure do now.

My name is Zach and my dad and I live on the farm next door to the abandoned house. When I told Dad about seeing the girl in the doorway, and described her—about 18, kind of short with a sexy smile—he turned a greenish gray and dashed off down the road. I followed. She was still there, standing in plain view, but I was the only one who could see her. What was going on?

As soon as we got home, Dad explained. The ghost only I could see was named Sue Ellen, and she and her husband Gene had moved in next door when my dad was 16. Gene was older than Sue Ellen and he beat her. She and my dad became friends and he agreed to help her run away.

She came to our place late on the night that Dad was to take her to the bus depot, but Gene caught her as she was screaming and banging on the back door. The shotgun blast caught her in the back and she died right there at our door.

I had noticed the stain by the door, and now I knew it was a bloodstain. Sue Ellen came back every year and died again, leaving a new bloodstain. Dad had never seen her again in all those years, but I could see her. He thought we could play the whole thing all over again and make it come out differently, so that Sue Ellen didn't die. I didn't like the idea because I figured if you changed the past, the present and the future would change too. But that's what we did. How did it turn out? I tell you the whole story in "Something's Different"—read it and find out.

And that's only one of the shocking stories you'll find in *Short Circuits*.

—Marianne Tait Pridemore
San Jose Public Library, San Jose, CA

📖 A Short Wait Between Trains: A Collection of War Stories by American Writers

Edited by Robert Benard. Delacorte, 1991. 432p. Hardbound (ISBN 0-385-30486-2) $18.00. **Grades 9–12, adults. 4Q, 2P.**

How does a person cope with war and the death and destruction it brings? It's an eternal question, and the answers in these stories tell us that, in the end, it matters little what war, or when. People find different ways to keep themselves together. The line blurs between soldier and civilian, enemy or friend, because people are all beset by the same emotional turmoil.

The women in Eudora Welty's Civil War story, "The Burning" and the Vietnamese women in Jim Pitzen's "The

Village" distance themselves from the horrors of war by retreating into their own memories.

A young woman remains stoic in James Purdy's "You Reach for Your Hat" when she learns that her fiance will not be coming home. James Jones tells of the violent reaction of a soldier on graveyard detail, who refuses to let anyone help him bury his own brother in "Greater Love."

Philip Roth lends a note of humor in "Defender of the Faith," as he describes the boot-camp antics of a group of raw recruits. Smiles fade, though, when a battle-weary sergeant ends the story with a startling jolt of cruelty.

Who, then, is the enemy? In Ralph Ellison's "Flying Home," a black airman is injured while training near his base in Alabama. Wracked with pain, he must also endure skepticism and ridicule while awaiting aid.

Strong friendships can grow through suffering. Tim O'Brian leads us through revenge to respect in "Ghost Soldiers." But once you have finally found a friend, again there's the question: who is the enemy, and where?

—*Mark Anderson*
Fairfax County Public Library, Fairfax, VA

📖 2041

Jane Yolen. Delacorte, 1991. 222p. Hardbound (ISBN 0-385-30445-5) $16.00. **Grades 7–12. 3Q, 2P.**

What will the future be like? A world where delicious ice cream creations cost nothing, and losing the weight gained from eating them costs everything . . . .

What will the future be like? Kids growing up in special space habitats, hating the Earth that originally gave them and their parents birth . . . .

What will the future be like? Freedom of speech and freedom of expression are concepts so outrageous that those who advocate such things are shot on sight . . . .

Welcome to the world of 2041, the world of the future. What will the future be like? No one knows, but

you can discover some of the possibilities here, and see what life might be like for your grandchildren and great-grandchildren.

—*Nancy A. Weitendorf*
Oxford Lane Library, Oxford, OH

📖 Untold Tales

William J. Brooke. HarperCollins, 1992. 165p. Hardcover (ISBN 0-06-020271-8) $15.00. **Grades 5–12, adults. 4Q, 3P.**

Fairy tales usually begin with "Once upon a time" and end with "happily ever after." But what if that weren't the ending, after all?

Once upon a time there was a Frog Prince, and a Princess kissed him, and he turned into a handsome Prince, married the Princess, became King, and they all lived happily ever after. Or did they? What if the Queen (who used to be the Princess) was lonely for her Frog Prince, who teased her and played with her and made up rhymes for her? All the King did was be King, and he had gotten to be very boring. Is there any way she can get her Frog Prince back? And if she did, what would happen to the kingdom with no King to run it?

We've all heard the story of Beauty and the Beast—but what if physical perfection and hideous ugliness weren't dealt out in exactly the way Walt Disney did it? And if Beauty agreed to marry the Beast, what unexpected results might it have? Take a new look at this fairy tale, and perhaps discover what true beauty really was all along.

And how would a princess feel about a prince who arrived 25 years too late, all because he'd kissed another princess and gotten sidetracked? Do they have any chance for happily ever after?

These are fairy tales that aren't quite what you'd expect them to be, and that make you wonder, "What really did happen after 'and they lived happily ever after'?"

—*JRB*

Recommended
Whole Language Resources
from Teacher Ideas Press

SCIENCE THROUGH CHILDREN'S LITERATURE: An Integrated Approach

Carol M. Butzow and John W. Butzow

*The best book I have come across for the integration of science and literature–loaded with good ideas.–*Science and Children

Instructional units for more than 30 outstanding children's fiction books that are rich in scientific concepts, yet equally well known for their strong story lines and universal appeal. K-3.

1989 xviii, 234p. ISBN 0-87287-667-5
$24.50

MATH THROUGH CHILDREN'S LITERATURE: Activities That Bring the NCTM Standards Alive

Kathryn L. Braddon, Nancy J. Hall, and Dale Taylor

The National Council for Teachers of Mathematics (NCTM) has developed standards aimed at introducing mathematical concepts and relationships to children in very early grades, allowing them to develop a familiarity and comfort with these concepts as part of their everyday world. This unique resource will foster that learning by using children's literature as a springboard to help teachers lead children along the path to successful mathematical literacy. K-6.

1993 xviii, 218p.
ISBN 0-87287-932-1
$23.50

SOCIAL STUDIES THROUGH CHILDREN'S LITERATURE: An Integrated Approach

Anthony D. Fredericks
Illustrated by Rebecca N. Fredericks

This activity-centered approach to elementary social studies features children's picture books, such as *Ox-Cart Man, In Coal Country*, and *Jambo Means Hello*, that illustrate important social studies concepts. K-5.

1991 xviii, 192p. ISBN 0-87287-970-4
$24.00

MUSIC THROUGH CHILDREN'S LITERATURE: Theme and Variations

Donna B. Levene

Illustrated folk songs, rhythmic poems, stories with musical themes, and other picture books with a strong musical basis are used in this unique teacher resource to provide a springboard for learning about music and developing music appreciation. Lively activities involve singing, playing instruments, chanting, and movement with titles such as *Possum Comes a-Knockin', All Join In, There's a Hole in the Bucket, Ragtime Tumpie, Berlioz the Bear*, and *Follow the Drinking Gourd.* Perfect for both nonmusicians and seasoned music specialists. PreK-6.

Spring 1993 ca.120p.
ISBN 1-56308-021-4
$22.50

BOOKS THAT HEAL: A Whole Language Approach

Carolyn Mohr, Dorothy Nixon, and Shirley Vickers

A whole language approach to bibliotherapy, a sensitive method of using books to guide children through problem solving by helping them identify with others who have coped with similar situations. The books chosen address problems of today's students such as relationships, self-concept, differences, poverty, divorce, and death. 3-6.

1991 xiv, 283p. ISBN 0-87287-829-5
$23.50

CREATING AND MANAGING THE LITERATE CLASSROOM

Suzanne I. Barchers

An enlightened philosophy aided by imaginative and detailed lesson models.
–Instructional Media Communication Skills

Innovative and useful, this guide offers economical, classroom-tested techniques for making the transition to whole language or literature-based programs. Includes sound advice for acquiring materials economically, implementing programs, encouraging student independence, plus lists of resources and activities and readily usable materials for model reading, writing, and research units. K-6.

1990 xv, 187p. ISBN 0-87287-705-1
$23.00

To order or for a free catalog call
Teacher Ideas Press, Dept. 27
1-800-237-6124
or write to us at Dept. 27,
P.O. Box 6633, Englewood, CO 80155-6633

Talking with Talkers

By Patrick Jones, Branch Manager
Tecumsah Branch, Fort Wayne, Indiana, Public Library

Patrick is the only booktalker I know to have gotten a standing ovation from a group of librarians, most of whom were booktalkers themselves. It was at the 1991 summer ALA conference, and I was one of the first people to stand up. His performance had had all of us on the edges of our seats, securely in the palm of his hand. I had never seen him perform before (doing a talk to share a book with a committee doesn't count), and I was absolutely blown away—and very glad that he was a long-standing contributor to *BT* and *NBT*.

Patrick is tall, thin, lanky, with long flyaway hair and wire-rimmed glasses. When he is doing talks or perhaps passionately defending a controversial YA book that someone thinks is not appropriate for teenagers, the air around him fairly crackles with energy. He's willing to try anything to get kids involved with books. In fact, it's been that way since he started doing booktalks. He was a young adult librarian in Springfield, Massachusetts, when he found some books by "this Bodart person . . . ." Booktalking sounded like a good way to get teenagers into the library and to help him learn the collection, so he wrote some talks and scheduled a class to share them with. But, like many of us (myself included), he made a lot of mistakes. In fact, he says, "I did it all wrong. I talked to a senior class at a vo tech high school, who probably hadn't read anything for three years, and didn't particularly want to. I did material that was way too young, and I didn't prepare enough material, so there was an embarrassing 10 minutes of silence at the end of the class, when I asked if anyone had any questions, and of course no one did.

"As a result of that experience, I learned that I needed to have more information about the classes I was going to talk to, like their grades and reading levels. I also realized that it would be easier to talk to classes that had a reason to listen to me: they had to do a book report, the teacher required them to read one of the books I talked about, they needed extra credit, something. That's not always possible, but when I can, I prefer to talk to classes who have a vested interest in listening to me."

Patrick says he used to depend on gimmicks when he was just starting out. He was willing to do *anything* to get kids to listen to him, from dressing in jeans and a sweatshirt to leaping onto a desk as part of a scary talk. One girl was so scared she ran away from him! "Ninety-nine out of 100 librarians couldn't get away with it, but it seemed natural for me—and it worked. But I wouldn't do it now. These days I do talks in a suit and don't need to depend on gimmicks anymore. Now it's just me and the talks—and now that I know what I'm doing, it works."

One reason Patrick stopped using gimmicks was that they didn't always work, especially the ones that involved machinery. "I wrote a talk on *In Country* and timed it to Springsteen's 'Born in the USA,' the song that inspired the book. But it was a disaster—the kids listened to the song, and not to me." Another time, when he was speaking at a conference to a group of librarians, he did a talk on *The Girl in the Box*. He arranged for someone to turn out all the lights, and had had a typewriter brought on stage so he could pretend to be typing while he gave the talk. But unfortunately, it was an electric typewriter, and when a key stuck, and it began to go crazy, Patrick couldn't figure out what to do about it in the dark, and so had to shout his talk over the sound of the typewriter going crazy. "Another world-class disaster!"

"I love doing booktalks because, during the talks, kids have reactions that I can see, and those reactions are different every time I do a talk. I can do the same talk seven different times in one day, and get seven different reactions. It makes it seem like seven different talks. Their reactions make it for me!"

Patrick has three pearls of wisdom for beginners. First, fight for the chance to do booktalks in the schools. Stress to the person who doesn't want you to do talks that you'll meet more kids in one day of booktalks than you would in a month of reference desk duty. Be practical in your arguments about why you want to do it. (And don't forget to mention the increased circulation figures that result from booktalking!—**Ed.**) Second, have realistic expectations about your audiences. Don't think that the kids will stand in awe of you and think everything you do is wonderful. But don't think they'll fall asleep as soon as you start talking, either. Reality is somewhere in between. Third, think of booktalking as a performance. There's a setting, an audience, a performer, and something that needs to be performed. Don't think just about writing talks, but also about performing them. For Patrick, at one time, that meant jumping on a table. For you, it will mean something else. But whatever you do, do what is right for you, and make sure that it is interesting and entertaining for your audience.

Patrick is also an inveterate list maker, in both professional and private life, a trait he used when he did an alphabetical list of 26 booktalking hooks for *BT*. He's working on a second alphabet now, and has promised to share it with *NBT* when it is finished. Look for it in a future issue.

In the next issue, you'll meet Dorothy Davidson, a member of the first library school class I taught as a teaching assistant in the early 1980s. It was a trial for all of us, because most of the class members were far better teachers than I was at the time, but Dorothy toughed it out, and has been doing booktalks ever since!

The Last Word: Top 10 Reasons to Do Booktalks (with Apologies to David Letterman)

By Jeff Blair, Librarian
Olathe South High School, Olathe, Kansas

10. Add some nervous tension to your life.

Let's face it: As librarians, we lead a relatively sedentary lifestyle. Here's a ready-made chance to add a jolt of adrenaline to your life and at the same time rescue yourself from marshmallowdom.

9. Lose weight.

I don't know about you, but I feel like I work and sweat off a couple of pounds each time I have to get up in front of a group of students.

8. Keep those circulation figures up.

Hey, we're talking job security here, too. I can't think of a better way to get interest generated in a batch of titles than by booktalking them. Kids *are* looking for good books to read, and you can deliver them on a silver platter. (But make sure you have enough copies first. I still remember with a shudder my first year as a librarian, when I had one copy of a book and forty to fifty requests for it.)

7. Do some image breaking.

I try to shatter that old "librarian" image whenever I can. Despite the stares, I've stopped wearing my beard in a bun. I figure we need to take every opportunity to break out of the library and take the chance of embarrassing ourselves, to show that we are real people too, not just musty keepers of the books.

6. What a way to meet girls/guys!

You're up there in front of 20 to 30 kids, so something's bound to click with some of them. I find that students are far more apt to talk with me about books, their research, and life in general, if they've had that contact in their classroom. I may not remember them when they come into the library, but they sure do remember me.

5. It's an exposure to wildlife.

Especially if you're talking to a junior high class!

4. The gratitude and support of a faculty member.

Look at it from their point of view—most of the hour off! I remember one teacher whom I practically had to approach on my knees and beg permission to booktalk in her class. She introduced me with a "He's here to do something" and icily appraised me during the first hour. She was also the first (he says modestly) to come up and get the books after I was through. She's been an enthusiastic fan ever since, and encourages others in her department to invite me into their classes. When a teacher can see you making a difference with a class, there's no better advertising.

3. How else can you enrapture and bore simultaneously?

I never cease to be amused by those classes where one student is hanging on your every word, drool pooling on the floor in anticipation of getting hold of a book—and sitting next to that kid is someone catching 40 winks.

2. Get those creative juices flowing.

I approach a book somewhat differently when I'm trying to work up a talk for it. I think about it more while I search for a hook, the approach that makes the talk work, something that will capture the essence of what's there. As much as I've come to enjoy giving the talks, I still like writing them more. The satisfaction of nailing down a talk and knowing it's all that it can be is unsurpassed, except perhaps by sex and chocolate.

And the number one reason to do booktalks is (drum roll please, Anton):

1. Read, read, READ!

I love to read. Those who know me know that there's usually a book in my hand; in fact, I'm told I was born that way! If I have a stack of books that I have to prepare for a presentation, it's just another excuse to be reading. Who could ask for more?

Author Index

Title Index

Note: Nonfiction titles are marked with an asterisk (*).

Subject Index

Genre Index

Grade-Level Index

High School Titles

Paperbound Titles Index

Contributors' Index